UNLIMITED WEALTH

Also by Paul Zane Pilzer (with Robert Deitz)

Other People's Money:
The Inside Story of the S & L Mess

UNLIMITED WEALTH

THE THEORY AND PRACTICE OF ECONOMIC ALCHEMY

PAUL ZANE PILZER

CROWN PUBLISHERS, INC.

New York

Published by Crown Publishers, Inc., 201 East 50th Street, New York, New York 10022. Member of the Crown Publishing Group

CROWN is a trademark of Crown Publishers, Inc.

Manufactured in the United States of America

Library of Congress Cataloging-in-Publication Data

Pilzer, Paul Zane.
    Unlimited wealth : the theory and practice of economic alchemy
Paul Zane Pilzer.—1st ed.
      p.   cm.
    1. Economics. 2. Wealth. 3. Technological innovations.
I. Title.
HB71.P617 1990
330.1'6—dc20

90-41618
CIP

ISBN 0-517-58211-2

10 9 8 7 6 5 4 3 2 1

First Edition

To Donna Lynn Casey

CONTENTS

PREFACE

"ELIAS!" I only called my father by his first name when I was angry with him. "How could you give Tony another raise?" Tony, a Puerto Rican cutter whom we had trained and promoted from a floor sweeper, had missed two days last week, and we had to pay the guaranteed minimum, $1.65 per hour, to two pieceworkers who had no work to sew.

"I had to," he shrugged. "His wife had another baby. A boy this time. That's why he forgot to call in."

I was unimpressed. I felt that Tony, at twenty-four (only four years older than myself), shouldn't have *any* kids, let alone four already, and all living with him in the Bronx on only $200 a week.

"But Dad," I objected, "he cost us $75 last week just by not calling in, let alone what the buyer at Macy's is going to do to us when he finds out we didn't ship his order. Listen to me! Please! We're going broke and you're going around giving raises to people we should be firing. You just don't understand!"

"Don't speak like that," he said sympathetically. "You can't fire Tony . . . where would he go? He barely speaks English. He'd end up as a floor sweeper somewhere at minimum wage."

"But Dad, we can't make it anymore. You just don't understand, do you?"

"No son," he said, "you don't understand. It's not worth being in business if you can't extend a hand to people who haven't had all of your advantages. Go to Wharton next year. Study hard. Figure out how you can make your million bucks and how we can stay in business to make jobs for the Tonys of this world. Then *you'll* understand."

My father was a religious man. He firmly believed in a true and just God who had a reason for everything. To him, an Eastern European immigrant who had seen his homeland destroyed during the Holocaust, the tragedies and misfortunes of human existence were simply the parts of God's plan that we could not yet understand. His philosophy was perhaps best summed up in the Kaddish, the Hebrew prayer for the dead—the prayer that, as the son of a religious Jew, I recited every morning for a year following his death in 1979.

The Kaddish is recited in Aramaic, the spoken language of the Jewish people in ancient times; it was originally written in Aramaic so that every member of the community would understand it. Yet even more significant than the fact that the Hebrew prayer for the dead is not recited in Hebrew is the fact that this prayer for the dead contains no mention whatsoever of death. Rather, in the midst of sorrow the Kaddish affirms our belief in the meaningfulness of life itself and our faith in a just and true God . . . even if He moves in what may seem to us to be mysterious ways.

My father, who spent virtually his whole life working to support his family, viewed his own business shortcomings and society's economic problems as one and the same: both were the result of our failure to understand and utilize the tools that God had given us. Even while he was dying of cancer in 1979, he never wavered for a moment in his belief that God was just and that human suffering was part of a divine plan that we did not yet understand. He firmly believed, as Albert Einstein once said, that God does not play dice with the universe.

To a man like my father, it was inconceivable that God would allow people to multiply in the billions and yet deny them the ability to feed and shelter themselves. Yet, like a loving father, God would not simply hand over to his children everything they needed. Rather, He would give them the necessary tools and allow them to discover how to use the tools to take care of themselves.

I began my studies at Wharton Graduate Business School in 1975 with this belief: that human suffering and social injustice reflected nothing more than our failure to use the tools that God had given us. I remember my shock upon learning in my first class that the entire field of economics is based on the concept of scarcity—that is, that there is a finite amount of resources in the world—and that the best we can hope for is to figure out a better way of dividing them. Not only did this contradict everything I had seen as the upwardly mobile child of an immigrant, it contradicted my entire belief in a true and just God, for such a God would not have created a world of limited resources in which one person's gain would have to be another person's loss.

At Wharton, it seemed to me that the science of economics had advanced only to where the science of medicine was at the beginning of the nineteenth century. Before we discovered the underlying theories that explained bacterial infections, and thus inoculations and antibiotics, we knew from experience what few medicines and treatments worked—applications. However, without an underlying theory explaining why, we were unable to learn and grow from our experiences, and, more significantly, only a select few could afford what little medical care existed. Similarly, my professors were able to teach me what worked—in applications courses such as marketing, finance, and management—but were unable to teach me why—in theoretical courses such as micro- and macroeconomics.

I felt then that the underlying theories behind business, which are based on the classical economic concept of scarcity, were wrong. But I did not have a theory to substitute in their place. This began my fifteen-year quest for a business theory that could better explain the past and predict the future. And, more important, a business theory consonant with a just and true God, which would allow everyone, not just a select few, to share in a better and better world.

UNLIMITED WEALTH

INTRODUCTION

For the past four hundred years, virtually all practitioners of the dismal science we call economics have agreed on one basic premise: namely that a society's wealth is determined by its supply of physical resources—its land, labor, minerals, water, and so on. And underlying this premise has been another, even more profound, assumption—one supposedly so obvious that it is rarely mentioned: namely that the entire world contains a limited amount of these physical resources.

This means, from an economic point of view, that life is what the mathematicians call a zero-sum game. After all, if there are only limited resources, one person's gain must be another person's loss; the richer one person is, the poorer his neighbors must be.

Over the centuries, this view of the world has been responsible for innumerable wars, revolutions, political movements, government policies, business strategies, and possibly a religion or two.

Once upon a time, it may even have been true. But not anymore.

Whether or not we ever did, today we do not live in a resource-scarce environment. That may seem hard to believe, but the businessperson and the politician—as well as the butcher, the baker, and the candlestick maker—who continue to behave as if they were operating in the old zero-sum world will soon find themselves eclipsed by those who recognize the new realities and react accordingly.

What are these new realities? To put it simply, we live today in a world of effectively *unlimited* resources—a world of *unlimited* wealth. In short, we live in what one might call a new Alchemic world.

The ancient alchemists sought to discover the secret of turning base metals into gold; they tried to create great value where little existed before. But an analysis of their writings shows that they were on a spiritual as well as a monetary quest. They believed that by discovering how to make gold they could offer unlimited prosperity to all of God's children. And, although in our era the term *alchemy* is often equated with "false science" and fraud, the ancient alchemists were successful in their quest in a manner that they could not have anticipated.

Consider this: if the ancient alchemists had succeeded in fabricating gold, gold would have become worthless and their efforts would have been for naught. Yet, through their attempts to make gold, they laid the foundation for modern science, which today has accomplished exactly what the alchemists hoped to achieve: the ability to create great value where little existed before. We have achieved this ability through the most common, the most powerful, and the most consistently underestimated force in our lives today—technology.

In the alchemic world in which we now live, a society's wealth is still a function of its physical resources, as traditional economics has long maintained. But unlike the outdated traditional economist, the alchemist of today recognizes that technology controls both the definition and the supply of physical resources. In fact, for the past few decades, it has been the *backlog* of unimplemented technological advances, rather than unused physical resources, that has been the determinant of real growth.

Fifteen years ago the world was supposedly running out of oil. Virtually every economist predicted that the end of an era was at hand. The industrial nations would have to tighten their belts, garage their cars, turn off their air conditioners, and generally adjust to lower standards of living. Today, oil prices (adjusted for inflation) are lower than they have been at any time since the 1960s. (Indeed, in terms of productivity—for example, how far a dollar's worth of gasoline will take you—prices are lower than they've ever been.) What's more, petroleum supplies are overflowing and the West is enjoying its ninth straight year of economic expansion.

What happened? What proved the economists wrong in their prediction? In a word, Alchemy.

Through the magic of technology, we developed better methods of producing energy and more efficient ways of using it. By replacing $300 carburetors with $25 computerized fuel injectors, automobile manufacturers doubled the fuel efficiency of new cars. This effectively doubled the supply of gasoline, thus effectively increasing the supposedly fixed supply of oil. At the same time, we also began developing entirely new energy sources, next to which the breakthroughs of the last decade will pale by comparison.

The French historian Fernand Braudel once described technology as the queen that changes the world. We might go Braudel one better and describe technology as a modern-day Eve who *defines* the world.

Our ability to transform the raw materials of nature into the most elegant and sophisticated devices imaginable—to "make computers from dirt," as the mathematician Mitchell Feigenbaum recently put it—has so dramatically altered the rules that we are playing an entirely new game.

The most successful entrepreneurs of our time—H. Ross Perot, Sam Walton, Steven Jobs—have been playing this new game without necessarily understanding its principles. Indeed, without knowing it, our best and brightest investment bankers, for example, have been proving the fundamental alchemic notion that resources are less important than technology; or, to put it in financial terms, that fixed physical assets are less important than intellectual assets. A decade ago, when T. Boone Pickens revolutionized the leveraged buyout (LBO) business, the action was mainly in oil companies and other physical-resource–oriented firms. In 1989, by contrast, the biggest LBO in the United States was the Time-Warner deal, involving two companies whose assets are almost exclusively intangible and intellectual.

This book explains the new "game"—its origins, its nature, and its rules. It spells out just what these new realities mean to businesspeople and government policymakers—what kind of business strategies and public policies make sense in the alchemic world and what kind are obsolete. It discusses what we, as consumers and citizens affected by it all, can and should do to become active participants in the game so as to enhance not only our own lives and the lives of our children but our society as well.

The book first explains the Theory of Alchemy in Chapters 1 through 4—the reasons behind what has been going on in our lives and our societies over the past few decades. The book then examines the applications of this theory in Chapters 5 through 11—what can and should be going on in our lives and our societies once we understand the theory.

Underlying the Theory of Alchemy is the notion that technology has liberated us from the zero-sum game of traditional economics. Instead of finding better ways to slice up the same old pie, in the alchemic world you concentrate on baking a new pie big enough for all to share. In short, *an Alchemist creates wealth; an economist merely moves it around.*

The potential applications for this theory are as profound as they are widespread. Some of these applications include:

1. *The only enduring business is the business of change.*

In the zero-sum environment of traditional economics, the world is viewed as essentially a game of chess; the pieces move around, sometimes in very intricate and confusing patterns, but the board and the rules always stay the same. In the alchemic world, the board and the rules of the game change virtually every day. Thus, while the economist believes that the route to success lies in mastering a particular business and then coping with changing conditions, the Alchemist understands that his or her very business *is* change—that the vital industry he or she was thriving in yesterday will be obsolete tomorrow. Alchemists understand that the opportunities they chased into one field are more than likely to lead them quickly to another and another and another, and they are willing to pursue them.

For example, the nation's retailers began as dry-goods merchants who typically sold fairly predictable lines of products to their customers. Perhaps once or twice a year the merchant added a new item to his inventory. No longer. In today's alchemic world, whether they are selling clothing or consumer electronics, the successful descendants of the dry-goods merchant have developed systems and personnel capable of turning over their entire product line one or more times each year. Rather than merely supplying customers with more of what they bought yesterday, alchemic retailers are in the business of continuously educating their customers about completely new products, since they rarely carry a single product unchanged for more than one season.

2. *The market has no corners.*

The economist attempts to succeed by cornering the market in some valuable commodity. The Alchemist recognizes that in a world of unlimited resources, businesses based on the exploitation of scarcity are doomed.

OPEC learned this lesson the hard way. So did the Hunt brothers, when they tried to corner the silver market. Worried about rising prices, Kodak, the world's largest silver user, began developing new photographic emulsions that used less and less silver—and some that used none at all. Silver prices plunged and the Hunts were wiped out. The same thing happened with platinum. Demand for the rare metal soared when the Big Three U.S. automakers developed a platinum-based catalytic converter in response to new antipollution regulations. Speculators swarmed into the commodities markets buying platinum futures, only to be blindsided when Ford announced the development of a catalytic converter that used a substitute for platinum. As a result, the price for platinum dropped 30 percent in a single day.

3. *No business is an island.*

The economist attempts to succeed by developing, and then monopolizing, some new product, process, or technology. The Alchemist knows that if you have a product, process, or technology that works, sooner or later someone will find a way to do it better or cheaper or both. You will succeed if you accept this inevitable fact and move quickly to take advantage of your having been there first; you will fail if you try to fight it.

As we shall see in Chapter 3, although the Sony Corporation was the first to introduce its superior Beta format VCR, it lost out to rival JVC's inferior VHS format by trying to monopolize rather than profitably share its new technology. And, as we shall also see in Chapter 3, IBM's inferior PC became the industry standard over Apple's superior MacIntosh product for the same reason.

4. *The first law of modern business is no longer "find a need and fill it," but "imagine a need and create it."*

Virtually our entire modern economy is built on the idea that increasing affluence has effectively erased the distinction between luxuries and necessities. Add to this technology's ability to create increasingly astonishing tools and toys, and you have a prescription for a world in which consumer appetite for new products is unlimited. Traditional marketing philosophy has been turned on its head, for today the product often precedes the need. In the alchemic world, new products create their own demand by changing the way people behave. To put it another way, existing markets are, or very soon will be, dying markets. By the end of the decade, the majority of successful businesspeople will no longer be supplying consumers with products that are simply better at filling existing needs; rather, they will be creating entirely new needs to fill.

As explained in Chapter 1, when Henry Ford introduced the cheap automobile, there was no need for such a product until availability of the affordable auto changed American life-styles to such an extent (opening up the suburbs, for example) that cars became a basic necessity of life. Similarly, when facsimile machines were introduced in the early 1980s there was relatively little demand for them until their availability made them as ubiquitous as the typewriter, a staple of the office necessary to the daily conduct of business.

5. *Labor is capital.*

The economist views labor as an inescapable cost of doing business; the trick is to get the best workers for the lowest wages. The Alchemist sees labor as *capital*— an asset ripe for investment. He or she recognizes that the return one gets from one's supply of labor is entirely dependent on how much one is willing to invest in it—specifically, in the form of education and training. Indeed, just as a society's wealth depends much more on technology than on its physical resources, so too does a worker's productivity depend much more on his or her education and training than on innate intelligence.

For example, when McDonald's decided to start opening inner-city franchises in the late 1960s and early 1970s, conventional economic wisdom held that the effort was bound to fail. Success in the fast-food business was heavily dependent on the availability of highly motivated and productive workers, very few of whom, it was believed, were to be found in the inner cities. What the experts didn't envision, however, was McDonald's willingness and ability to expand its traditional training programs to include motivational courses to teach potential employees the meaning and importance of the work ethic and its rewards.

McDonald's had recognized the problem: society hadn't sufficiently invested in the inner-city labor force to teach this concept. It closed the educational gap and got the workers it needed.

The alchemic world is neither a promising model, a hypothetical theory, nor an abstract dream. The alchemic world has arrived; we are living in it right now. Indeed, almost all of our successful people are applying its principles, though they may not know its underlying formulas. Alchemy explains *why* their behavior is so effective. But, more important, it explains to would-be achievers how the alchemic view can lead them to success. And, like any good theory, it not only explains the recent past and the present but also provides a guidepost for the future.

THE THEORY OF ALCHEMY

In which we introduce a new and more accurate way of looking at the world: the alchemic reality of unlimited wealth.

FOR ANCIENT peoples, the key to human destiny was to be found in the heavens—the mysterious shining objects that wheeled across the sky each day and night. On the most profound level, the celestial dome served as a distant and apparently fixed screen against which people could measure their existence and ponder their future. More practically, it provided them with a reliable guidepost for their daily affairs. The sun told humans when to get up and when to retire. The moon influenced the tides and echoed the reproductive cycles of women. And the relative positions of sun, moon, and planets marked the changing of the seasons, signaling when it was time to sow and when to reap.

Until roughly the fourth century B.C., common belief held that the mysterious lights in the sky were gods wandering about the heavens. (Indeed, the word *planet* came from the Greek word for "wanderer.") In 340 B.C., however, Aristotle came up with the first modern theory of the universe, asserting that the planets and every other object in the heavens were in fact spheres that revolved in fixed paths around a stationary earth. Some 450 years later, Ptolemy developed a mathematical framework to support Aristotle's geocentric theory. As a result of Ptolemy's work, for the first time human beings could predict what was going to happen in the physical world and plan accordingly.

The Aristotelian-Ptolemaic concept of a universe in which every-thing revolved around a stationary earth remained the bedrock of Western thought for nearly two millennia. Its endurance was hardly surprising. For one thing, it accorded with the evidence of one's senses. After all, from your vantage point on earth, it certainly looks as if everything revolves around you. What's more, it agreed with our theology. Created as we were in the image and likeness of the one true God, where else would people expect to abide but in the center of creation?

In the early sixteenth century, however, a Polish astronomer named Nicolaus Copernicus came up with what seemed to be a more accurate way of looking at the cosmos—accurate, that is, in the sense that it produced more reliable astronomical predictions than Aristotle's geo-centric model. In the process, Copernicus displaced the earth—and humankind along with it—from the center of existence. According to Copernicus, it was the sun—not the earth—around which the heavenly bodies revolved.

Understandably fearful of being branded a heretic, Copernicus cir-culated his heliocentric model anonymously, presenting it merely as an improved method of making astronomical predictions, rather than as a new celestial order. His *De Revolutionibus Orbium Caelestium* was not published until he was on his deathbed in 1543, and his work was not taken seriously for well over half a century.

This changed in 1609, when the Italian mathematician and physicist Galileo Galilei began observing the heavens through a new invention known as the telescope. One of the first things Galileo observed was that the planet Jupiter had several moons revolving around it. To Galileo, the implications of this discovery were clear: not everything in the sky revolved around the earth. In other words, Copernicus might be right. Quickly confirming his hypothesis with additional observa-tions, Galileo wrote a treatise about Copernicus' theory—in colloquial Italian, rather than the traditional Latin of academia—that soon at-tracted wide support for the heliocentric model of the universe.

The bulk of that support, however, came from outside the establish-ment. The reaction from inside was quite different. Galileo was quickly and bitterly attacked by both Aristotelian scholars and Roman Catholic theologians. In 1616, the church commanded him never again to "hold, teach, or defend the Copernican system in any way whatever."

Sixteen years later, emboldened by his longtime friendship with Pope Urban VIII, Galileo challenged the ban by publishing his famous *Dialogues,* a hypothetical discussion of heliocentric theory. The church reacted swiftly. In 1633, Galileo was tried and convicted of heresy. Though his friendship with Urban VIII probably saved him from being burned at the stake, he was nonetheless sentenced to house arrest and his works were placed on the Vatican's Index of Forbidden Books, where they would remain for the next two hundred years.

Though Galileo and Aristotle held diametrically opposed views of the nature of the physical universe, they had in common something much more profound. Both believed that it was within humankind's power to understand how the world works and, by doing so, gain some measure of control over its destiny.

Today, the belief in our ability to understand, and thus control, our lives is accepted throughout the civilized world, though our sense of the particular understanding we need in order to exercise such control has changed considerably over the millennia. Ancient people, concerned as they were mainly with agricultural production, sought to control their environment by learning to understand the motion of celestial objects, in order to better predict the changing of the seasons. Modern people, at least in the industrialized West, have quite different priorities. They are primarily concerned with maximizing the value of their labor and thus their ability to earn money—in short, with what we call economic issues. As a result, they seek to control their environment by learning to understand economic cycles, rather than celestial mechanics.

It is thus hardly surprising that so many of the great minds in recent history have concerned themselves with economic matters. Indeed, they have come to regard economic theory in precisely the same way the ancient philosophers viewed the heavens—as the key to understanding and controlling our fate. As John Maynard Keynes noted in 1936, "the ideas of economists . . . are more powerful than is commonly understood. Indeed, the world is ruled by little else. Practical men, who believe themselves to be quite exempt from any intellectual influences, are usually the slaves of some defunct economist."[1]

---

[1]John Maynard Keynes, *The General Theory of Employment, Interest, and Money,* Harvest/HBJ ed. (San Diego: Harcourt Brace Jovanovich, 1964), 383. Keynes' great work was first published in England in 1936.

There is much to be said for according economics such importance in the modern world. Certainly, recent developments in the Soviet Union and Eastern Europe have made clear that, over the long run, what enables governments to maintain power is not force of arms but their ability to meet the economic needs of their people. The history of the past few decades yields convincing evidence—from the postwar renaissance of Japan to the global ubiquity of Coca-Cola and Levis— that the ultimate source of military might, political clout, and even cultural influence is nothing more or less than economic power.

For nearly two thousand years, from Aristotle's day to the time of Galileo, astronomers defined their discipline as the study of the fixed spheres that revolved around the earth. It is therefore not surprising that it took so long until Copernicus realized that the earth actually revolved around the sun. After all, the astronomers' definition of their own work precluded this hypothesis from consideration.

The study of economics has been hindered by this same sort of tunnel vision.

For the past four hundred years, ever since the earliest days of what we have come to call the dismal science, virtually all economists have agreed on one basic premise: a society's wealth is determined by its supply of physical resources—its land, labor, minerals, water, and so on. Underlying this common belief is another, even more profound, assumption: the world contains only a limited amount of these physical resources.

The world's most popular textbook on the dismal science, Paul Samuelson's classic *Economics*, defines the science it aims to teach as follows:

> Economics is the study of how people and society choose to employ *scarce* resources that could have alternative uses in order to produce various commodities and to distribute them for consumption.[2] [emphasis added]

To be sure, other books define economics differently. But virtually all definitions of the subject—and the work of virtually all of the great

[2]Paul Samuelson and William D. Nordhaus, *Economics*, 12th ed. (New York: McGraw-Hill, 1985), 4.

economists, from Adam Smith to Karl Marx to John Maynard Keynes—share one term in common. Although their methodologies might differ, all view economics as a means of understanding how society uses and distributes *scarce* resources.

Since World War II, the wealth of the Western world has been expanding at an unprecedented pace, confounding the expectations of conventional economic theories. Unable to explain this activity, economists have taken to qualifying their predictions and prescriptions with phrases such as "on the other hand, . . ." a state of affairs that once led Harry Truman to remark that what the United States needed was a good one-handed economist.

In particular, economists have been baffled by the sustained expansion that the U.S. economy has enjoyed throughout the 1980s. Our continued economic growth, and the resulting increase in real wealth for the entire Western world, cannot be explained by any traditional economic theory predicated on the concept of a scarce supply of resources. In a very real sense, we are in the same position as Galileo was when he pointed his telescope at the moons of Jupiter. And, just as Galileo's observation led him to reexamine Aristotle's geocentric model of the universe, so too does the recent and apparently inexplicable sustained growth of the U.S. economy lead us to examine economic theory in a new light.

What that new observation reveals may, at first glance, seem as unbelievable as what Galileo saw in his primitive telescope. We live today in a world of unlimited, not scarce, resources—a world of unlimited wealth. In short, we live in the alchemic world.

In the alchemic world, a society's wealth is still a function of its physical resources, as traditional economics has always maintained. But unlike the obsolete economist, the new Alchemist recognizes that today both the definition and the supply of those physical resources are controlled—almost exclusively—by technology. In fact, for the past few decades, it is the backlog of unimplemented technological advances, rather than the supply of unused physical resources, that has been the determinant of real growth.

In 1981, urged on by newly elected President Ronald Reagan, the U.S. Congress passed the Economic Recovery Tax Act (ERTA), which dramatically lowered individual income tax rates and provided tax incentives to businesses that purchased new equipment. As put forth by the supply-siders who then dominated the Reagan administration's economic policymaking councils, the idea behind the legislation was that the increased work incentive resulting from lower tax rates would lead to increased economic activity, which in turn would more than offset the reductions in federal revenue that tax cuts might normally be expected to produce. This was something of a radical notion. Indeed, many traditional economists warned that Reagan's policy would lead to an economic collapse; they expected federal deficits to balloon without the expected corresponding increase in gross national product (GNP).[3]

But that's not what happened. Late in 1982, the GNP began a meteoric rise that initially outstripped even the most optimistic projections of the supply-siders.

Not surprisingly, the supply-siders took full credit for the boom, and in 1984 Reagan was reelected by the greatest landslide in U.S. history. The fact was, however, that by 1984, with the federal deficit also growing at a record rate, the supply-siders were starting to worry about the validity of their theories. Many of them began predicting that unless the spiraling budget deficit could somehow be checked, the nation would face severe inflation, escalating interest rates, and economic stagnation.

The economy, however, paid no heed to such warnings. From 1985 through 1988, the budget deficit continued to increase, nearly doubling the national debt. Yet, despite dire predictions to the contrary, GNP continued to grow unabated. Indeed, by 1989 most economists, ignoring their earlier concerns, were expecting the economy to continue its climb well into the 1990s, although they were unable to support their projections with a specific explanation or theory. Clearly, something was going on that not even the supply-siders—the ones supposedly responsible for the boom—could explain. It was, in fact, Alchemy at work.

The expansion of the past decade had its genesis in 1946, when the first electronic computer, known as ENIAC, was developed at the

[3]*Gross national product* is defined as the value, at current market prices, of all final goods and services produced within some period by a nation (without any deduction for depreciation of capital goods). From Paul Samuelson and William D. Nordhaus, *Economics,* 906.

University of Pennsylvania. Over the next thirty-five years, even though computers became progressively smaller, faster, more powerful, and easier to use, their use remained generally restricted to the sterile and carefully guarded data-processing centers of universities, government agencies, and large corporations. By 1981, however, the computer had evolved to the point where it was ready to burst out into the wider world, onto the factory floor, inside the automobile, and onto the supermarket checkout counter. It was merely coincidence that Reagan's Economic Recovery Tax Act was enacted at the very moment the computer made its move into the productive sector of the economy.

The tax incentives that ERTA gave businesses in 1981—in effect, a government subsidy amounting to 58 percent of the cost of new equipment—virtually forced corporate America to retool.[4] Among other things, this greatly accelerated the integration of the computer throughout the economy. The short-term effect of wholesale computerization was an increase in productivity—or, to put it in alchemic terms, growth in the relative levels of implemented technology—on a scale not seen since the dawn of the industrial revolution.

The impact of these massive productivity increases was both immediate and profound. To begin with, by significantly lowering the production cost of virtually all goods and services, they reduced inflation. In addition, by swelling corporate profits, they effectively expanded the supply of capital, which in turn kept interest rates down. And finally, they gave the United States eight years of unprecedented economic growth. In fact, the effect of this technological change on inflation, interest rates, and GNP has been so significant that it has more than compensated for the continuing growth of the federal budget deficit and the massive increase in military spending. Moreover, an alchemic analysis of the 1981–89 period shows that these increases are only the beginning of a multidecade period of economic expansion for the entire industrialized world.

The reason for this impressive growth has to do with the *technology gap.* When traditional economists talk about a technology gap, they are generally referring to the disparity in technological sophistication between the United States and Japan, or between the industrialized nations and the Third World. In the Theory of Alchemy, by contrast,

[4]Paul Zane Pilzer, "The Real Estate Business and Technological Obsolescence," *Real Estate Review* (Fall 1989), 30–33.

the technology gap is not between countries but between the best technology currently available and any less-advanced technology actually in use. In the alchemic equation, the size of the technology gap—that is, the amount of available but unimplemented technology—is the greatest determinant of economic growth. And our technology gap today is wider than it has ever been in the history of civilization, owing to the types of technological advances we have been experiencing.

The speed at which technology advances is primarily determined by the speed at which we exchange and process information. This is because virtually all modern advances in technology are dependent on other technological advances. For example, the development of the fuel-efficient automobile was dependent on the development of computerized fuel injection, which in turn was dependent on the development of the computer, which in turn was dependent on developments in many other areas, such as semiconductors and circuit design. Each new technological advance makes possible a whole series of future technological advances. What determines the speed at which these advances occur is the speed at which the millions of scientists and engineers working on thousands of interrelated projects can access and share information about each other's breakthroughs. Thus, in a very real sense, the technology of information processing is the throttle on the engine of general technological advance.

Of all the enormous technological gains we have witnessed in recent years, advances in information-processing technology have been the most impressive. In fact, the science of information processing has reached a state of critical mass—breakthroughs in today's computers come directly from yesterday's breakthroughs, computer programs write other programs, and computers actually design computers that design other computers. The multiplier effect of information-processing technology has caused an explosive advance, which has led to an ever-growing backlog of unimplemented resource technology. As a result, despite the meteoric rise in GNP over the past decade, we have barely scratched the surface of what is currently possible and what is about to become possible.

Historically, we measured levels of technology in terms of ages: the Iron Age, the Bronze Age, and so on. More recently, our yardstick was revolutions, such as the agricultural or industrial revolutions, which generally played themselves out over several decades. In the early

1960s, we began speaking of product generations, which usually spanned a few years.

Today, technology is changing by the moment. As a result, the snapshot provided by traditional economic theories can no longer give us an accurate picture of economic activity, let alone predict future activity. The view of technology provided by traditional economic theories is as out of date as the traditional definition of physical resources. Today there is a dynamic, exponential relationship between the continuing advance of information-processing technology and the pace at which other technologies develop. The effect is not only an expansion of our supply of resources, but constant change in the definition of what constitutes a resource. To put it another way, information-processing technology has a multiplier effect on the various resource-oriented technologies, which in turn have a multiplier effect on each other and on overall wealth. As a result, real wealth is not only expanding faster than ever before, but it is surpassing society's apparently insatiable appetite to consume the new riches that are constantly being produced in greater and greater quantities.

Traditional economists have generally ignored the impact of technology on economic growth because traditional economics has always treated technology as a constant. To be fair, there have been exceptions, among them such major figures as Joseph A. Schumpeter, who argued that technical innovation is the driving force behind the alternating cycles of boom and bust; John Kenneth Galbraith, who introduced the concept of the technostructure; and Robert M. Solow, who won the Nobel Prize for his work showing that the difference between slow- and fast-growing economies was not the rate of capital accumulation but technology. But none of these men formulated the three major tenets of the Theory of Alchemy:

• Technology is the major determinant of wealth because it determines the nature and supply of physical resources.

• The advance of technology is determined mainly by our ability to process information.

• The backlog of unimplemented technological advances (that is, the technology gap) is the true predictor of economic growth for both the individual and society.

Technology doesn't just affect the supply side of the economic equation. It has an even more impressive impact on the demand side.

In the 1930s, Lord Keynes predicted that some day everyone would have a four-bedroom house, at which point, the American dream having been fulfilled, people would lose their incentive to work. Keynes believed that peoples' affluence would eventually outstrip their appetites—that their demand for goods and services would reach a plateau, beyond which the amount of money they spent would represent a smaller and smaller percentage of their income. Therefore, he argued, the government would have to adopt fiscal policies designed to keep people from hoarding too much of their income.[5]

Today, we know that nothing could be further from the truth. Indeed, the very opposite of what Keynes predicted seems to have come to pass. As evidenced by the spending habits of the contemporary yuppie, upscale consumer demand is insatiable. The more we earn, the more we spend; the more we spend, the more we get; the more we get, the more we want; and the more we want, the harder we seem to be willing to work to earn more money to get it. If any segment of our society has lost the incentive to work, it is the poor, not the upwardly mobile and increasingly wealthy middle class.

What has happened to confound Keynes' prediction that increasing affluence will lead to decreasing consumption? In part, Keynes got tripped up by a basic misunderstanding of human psychology. Improving prospects breed rising expectations, not complacency. Thus, as John Kenneth Galbraith noted in 1958, "In the affluent society, no sharp distinction can be made between luxuries and necessaries."[6]

Galbraith, of course, was talking mainly about consumer psychology—as used by advertisers to play on consumers' insecurities, envy, and self-esteem to make them want things they don't really need; or as imposed by consumers upon themselves. (Consider, for example, how the acquisition of a luxurious new suit makes a consumer feel that he must have an equally luxurious silk tie, a fine linen shirt, and a pair of Italian leather shoes to match.)

The fact is, technology does more than alter a consumer's sense of

[5]Keynes, *The General Theory of Employment, Interest, and Money.*

[6]John Kenneth Galbraith, *The Affluent Society,* 4th revised ed. (New York: New American Library, 1958), 226.

entitlement. It provides us with an ever-increasing array of astonishing new products, the use of which changes our behavior to such an extent that before long what we initially regarded as a luxurious new toy or tool becomes essential to our way of life.

For example, when Henry Ford introduced the cheap automobile, there was no need for such a product. Within a few decades, however, the availability of the auto had profoundly altered American life-styles —among other things, by prompting millions of people to move to the suburbs. As a result, by the early 1950s the family car had become a necessity.

Similarly, upon the introduction of facsimile machines in the early 1980s there was relatively little demand for them. But as technology lowered their price and uses for the product became apparent, the number of fax machines in use increased dramatically, and before long fax machines became a necessity for survival in the business world. Just as the automobile, the luxury item of the 1920s, became the basic necessity of the 1950s, so too did the fax machine, the luxury of well-to-do banks and law firms in 1985, become the necessity of even the corner deli by 1988. (It's worth noting, by the way, that the time it takes a massive behavioral change to transform a luxury into a necessity has shrunk from three decades to three years—and may soon be down to three months.)

Virtually our entire modern economy is based on this eroding distinction between luxuries and necessities. In today's alchemic world, individual wealth is created not merely by figuring out how to supply an existing product at a lower price, but more often by creating an entirely new product, filling a need that consumers didn't even know they had. In this light, it is hardly surprising to discover that many of the greatest personal fortunes acquired in modern times—for example, those of H. Ross Perot (data-processing), Sam Walton (automated distribution), and Steven Jobs (personal computers)—were created by individuals who supplied society with products and services that did not even exist when they were born.

Though only dimly perceived, the new alchemic reality is already taking hold in the United States and abroad. The world may not yet understand exactly how modern wealth is largely a function of technology, but the critical importance of technology—and the corresponding decline in the significance of traditionally defined physical resources—is beginning to dawn on leaders in both business and government. Indeed, this slow-growing realization has already led to a number of major changes in the foreign and domestic policies of many nations.

Before World War II, when technology was still advancing at a relatively slow pace, conventional wisdom held that the only way for a nation to increase its wealth was through the conquest and control of another nation's physical resources. Today, most nations recognize that this is no longer the case. After all, the island-nation of Japan, with very limited physical resources, today enjoys the world's highest per capital GNP, while the enormous empire of the Soviet Union, which boasts the world's largest supply of physical resources, has one of the lowest per capita GNPs. Clearly, the key to riches today is advancing technology, not the accumulation of physical resources.

One of the most significant effects of this change has been the decline in the value of military power in the alchemic world. Japanese military expenditures as a percentage of GNP are among the lowest in the world, while those of the Soviets are among the highest. Indeed, conquering another nation today is hardly an effective means of enhancing the aggressor nation's wealth. While it may yield some physical resources, sheer might will not control technological innovation, which in today's alchemic world is infinitely more valuable.

The recent changes in Soviet policy, both foreign and domestic, seem to reflect some awareness of the alchemic equation—or at least a realization that technology, not physical resources, holds the key to increasing real wealth. For one thing, as evidenced by their recent withdrawal from Afghanistan and the release of their grip on Eastern Europe, the Soviets seem to be backing away from the traditional Soviet doctrine of geographic expansion. For another, as part of an attempt to reform their domestic economy, they have embarked upon a restructuring program *(perestroika)* that recognizes both the supply and demand sides of the alchemic equation. *Perestroika* seeks to increase productivity by providing economic incentives, and by making consumer goods available for those who use the incentives to earn extra rubles. Of course, a full year before *perestroika,* the Soviets stunned the world by implementing the policy known as *glasnost,* the apparent opening of their society to the free exchange of information. The genius of Mikhail Gorbachev may lie in his realization that in order to have *perestroika* (alchemic economic reform), he first needed *glasnost* (the free exchange of information).

In the early nineteenth century, the economist David Ricardo asserted that the wealth of a nation was determined by its available farmland, and that an inevitable scarcity of land would eventually put an end to economic growth. Thomas Malthus, a clergyman who pioneered both economics and demography, argued that as the wealth of the working class increased, so too would its birth rate, increasing the number of people who must share the wealth and dooming the society to live forever at a subsistence level. Indeed, Malthus regarded war, famine, and pestilence as "positive" checks on population growth. A half-century after Malthus, Karl Marx put forth the notion that capitalism could not function if workers were well paid, and that the continued and inevitable exploitation of labor would eventually lead to world revolution and the demise of capitalism. More recently, John Maynard Keynes postulated that increasing affluence would lead to a proportionate decline in consumption, and that only government intervention designed to limit and redistribute income could maintain full employment.

Each of these viewpoints made sense at the time, and all helped people understand and take some control of their environment. But then again, so too did the cosmology of Aristotle and Ptolemy. Indeed, by regarding technology as a constant in the economic firmament, by assuming that the supply of resources was fixed and hence scarce, Ricardo, Malthus, Marx, Keynes, and all their followers were unwittingly mimicking the ancient astronomers who believed that the earth was the center of the universe. Just as those who followed the ancient astronomers realized that the geocentric model of the universe didn't fit their observations, we are beginning to realize that traditional economic theory does not fit what we observe around us. We are beginning to realize that the classic assumption of scarcity must give way to the dynamic calculus of effectively unlimited physical resources.

In agriculture today it makes far more sense to try to triple the yield of your farmland than to triple the size of your farm. Of course, before the advent of irrigation and pesticides—and, most recently, the advances in genetic engineering that have allowed biologists to create plants that require less water and are less vulnerable to pests—such a strategy was not feasible.

Similarly, in the oil industry today it is far better, both economically and environmentally, to increase fuel efficiency than to find, obtain, distribute, and store additional supplies of fuel. But, before the recent breakthroughs in computer-controlled combustion, this strategy, too, was not feasible.

And, perhaps most important, when it comes to labor we are discovering that it makes infinitely more sense to produce more productive members of society by investing early in their education and training than to transfer wealth from those who are producing more and more to those who are producing less and less.

In a December 1965 cover story on the enormous influence the theories of John Maynard Keynes had come to have on U.S. business-people and government policymakers, *Time* magazine quoted Milton Friedman, the leading monetary economist of the day and a future Nobel laureate, as declaring, "We are all Keynesians now."[7] Friedman may have been right at the time, but it is no longer so. As the twentieth century draws to a close, we are all Alchemists now.

[7]"The Economy: 'We Are All Keynesians Now'," *Time*, 31 December 1965, 65.

SUPPLY-SIDE ALCHEMY: $W = PT^n$

In which we define the First Law of Alchemy, which explains how technology determines the nature of physical resources; the Second Law of Alchemy, which explains how technology determines the supply of physical resources; and, most important of all, the Third Law of Alchemy, which explains what controls the advance of technology—and hence contains the key to wealth.

IN THE EARLY 1970s, pessimism was the order of the day. The world, it was said, was running out of everything. Unless radical action was taken immediately—action that included massive conservation efforts and a wholesale lowering of Western standards of living—humanity was doomed.

At bottom, this apocalyptically gloomy view of things was probably nothing more than an understandable reaction to the optimism of the previous decade. Nonetheless, it did have a specific genesis: the publication early in 1972 of *The Limits to Growth*, an enormously influential—and utterly downbeat—study issued by the Club of Rome, a collection of distinguished industrialists, scientists, economists, sociologists, and government officials from twenty-five countries.[1]

The Club of Rome had commissioned the study three years earlier, recruiting a team of seventeen experts—ranging from an Iranian popu-

[1]The Club of Rome, *The Limits to Growth* (New York: Universe Books, 1972).

22

lation analyst to a Norwegian pollution specialist—to peer down the road a bit and report back on the economic and environmental prospects. Working first under the direction of futurist Jay Forrester of the Massachusetts Institute of Technology, and then under Forrester's colleague, MIT business professor Dennis Meadows, the experts used some of the most sophisticated computer modeling techniques then available to produce a 197-page report that came to a genuinely shocking conclusion. What their computer models told them was that with the world's population growing at a rate of about 2 percent a year and industrial output rising by 7 percent annually, the world's physical resources would be exhausted sometime in the next few decades—a calamity, they said, that could wind up wiping out most of humanity before the year 2100.

The study's impact was phenomenal. For as long as anyone could remember, economic growth had been regarded as the solution to all of humankind's woes; now, suddenly, it seemed to be the problem. Thinking big was deemed archaic, if not downright antisocial. The party was over; it was time for people everywhere to pull up their socks and lower their expectations. You might not like it, but what could you do? The Club of Rome wasn't a bunch of antisocial hippies, but an organization of some of the most highly regarded businesspeople, researchers, and intellectuals of the day. And their conclusions seemed so scientific. As *Time* magazine noted: "Meadows is no latter-day Malthus prophesying doom on the basis of intuition: instead he has produced the first vision of the apocalypse ever prepared by a computer."[2]

To be sure, not everyone was persuaded by *The Limits to Growth* that the sky was falling. There were more than a few skeptics who scoffed at the Club of Rome's cheerless projections as misleading and shortsighted. But most such doubts were washed away the following year when Arab oil producers responded to the 1973 Yom Kippur war in the Middle East first by unilaterally raising prices and then by cutting off deliveries to the West. Though the actual embargo didn't last very long, the price hikes stuck—in the process, establishing the Organization of Petroleum Exporting Countries (OPEC) as a force to be reckoned with. They also marked what at the time seemed to be the

[2]"Can the World Survive Economic Growth?" *Time*, 14 August 1972, 56.

end of the era of cheap and abundant energy—an era that most people took to be synonymous with prosperity and growth.

What followed over the next few years seemed to prove the doomsayers right. Between 1973 and 1981, soaring energy prices pitched the United States headlong into its worst recession in four decades. Economic growth sputtered to a halt, unemployment mounted, and inflation soared, seemingly out of control. Long lines became commonplace at gas stations, with frustrated motorists often coming to blows. Electrical brown-outs became a regular feature of urban summers, and with heating oil deliveries uncertain, nervous New England homeowners turned down their thermostats in winter.

The future looked grim indeed. Americans, we were told, would have to tighten their belts, garage their cars, turn off their appliances, and generally adjust to lower standards of living. The government even printed up millions of gasoline ration cards. As David Rockefeller observed in 1975, there seemed no getting around the fact that there were now "constraints on the rate of economic growth, constraints that were not apparent in the preceding twenty years."[3]

In short, it looked as if the world we had known—the world of expansion and prosperity, of thinking big and rising expectations—was coming to an end. In its place, a new image came to dominate our thinking: that of the earth as a fragile spaceship with a rapidly declining store of supplies and fuel. And the consensus was that we had better get used to it. "The idea of sitting still until this thing blows over is just a bunch of nonsense," declared the president of Booz, Allen & Hamilton, Inc., one of the nation's largest management-consulting firms, in 1975. "It ain't gonna blow over. You can bet that for the next generation we're going to have to live with the conditions we've seen over the last decade."[4]

But then a strange thing happened. The world didn't come to an end.

As we approach the final years of the twentieth century, we are coming to grips with an astonishing—and heartening—realization. The Club of Rome scientists and the other environmental pessimists

[3]Allan Mayer and William J. Cook, "Thinking Small," *Newsweek*, 2 June 1975, 56.
[4]Mayer and Cook, "Thinking Small," 60.

of the 1970s were wrong. The world's supply of physical resources is not decreasing. On the contrary, our effective supply of resources is increasing.

Consider the example of one of our world's most essential and problematic resources—crude oil.

On the eve of the 1973 oil crisis, global oil reserves were figured to be something on the order of 700 billion barrels—enough to last about forty years at then current rates of consumption.[5] If the pessimists were right, over the next fifteen years those reserves should have dwindled to about 500 billion barrels. Well, the pessimists were wrong. In 1987, worldwide oil reserves were estimated at close to 900 billion barrels—nearly 30 percent *more* than they'd been fifteen years earlier. And that 900 billion barrel figure included only proven reserves; it didn't count the nearly *2,000* billion additional barrels of oil still waiting to be discovered or produced by enhanced recovery methods.[6]

The same is true of most other commodities. In 1970, worldwide natural gas reserves were estimated to total some 1,500 trillion cubic feet. By 1987, that estimate had been revised upward to nearly 4,000 trillion cubic feet. Similarly, global reserves of copper more than doubled (from 279 million to 570 million tons) between 1970 and 1987. Over the same period, silver reserves climbed more than 60 percent (from 6.7 billion to 10.8 billion troy ounces), gold reserves rose by 50 percent (from 1 billion to 1.52 billion troy ounces), and bauxite reserves were up more than 35 percent (from 17 billion to 23 billion metric tons).[7] The list goes on.

As supplies have increased, prices have tumbled. Between 1980 and 1985 alone, prices in the International Monetary Fund's thirty-product commodity index dropped fully 74 percent. Throughout the 1980s, the cost of such raw materials as bauxite, coal, cocoa beans, coffee, copper, cotton, hides, iron ore, lead, manganese, nickel, oil, potash, rice, rub-

[5]James Cook, "We're Not Going to Freeze in the Dark," *Forbes,* 27 June 1988, 106.

[6]According to the National Energy Information Center in Washington, D.C., estimated world oil reserves totaled 889.5 billion barrels in 1987.

[7]All 1970 resource statistics from C. B. Reed, *Fuels, Minerals and Human Survival* (Ann Arbor: Ann Arbor Science Publishers, 1975). All 1987 oil and gas statistics from the National Energy Information Center in Washington, D.C. All other 1987 resource statistics from the *1990 World Almanac and Book of Facts.*

ber, silver, soybeans, sugar, tin, and wheat collapsed—many falling to their lowest level in half a century. And the outlook for the foreseeable future is for more of the same. Indeed, the downward trend has been so dramatic that the U.S. Office of Technology Assessment was led to conclude in a 1988 study that America's "future has probably never been less constrained by the cost of natural resources."[8]

Conventional economics has a simple explanation for this kind of situation. Increasing supplies and falling prices are traditionally regarded as classic symptoms of faltering demand and economic contraction—in other words, of recession and depression. Yet, economically speaking, the decade of the 1980s was anything but that. Indeed, as we have noted, in the United States and most of the rest of the industrialized world, the 1980s saw one of the biggest peacetime economic booms ever. Industrial output, real wages, standards of living—all rose steadily, in some case sharply, and are continuing to rise. (Although, as we shall see later on, not everyone is sharing equally in this rising prosperity.)

To put it simply, we are richer than we have ever been before. This may seem hard to believe in an era in which we seem to be overrun with poverty and crime, in which we often feel that we have to work harder than ever simply to make ends meet. But it's true. Though it may sometimes seem as if we're trapped in the Red Queen's race—having to run faster and faster merely to stay in the same place—the fact is that we have to work significantly less than we used to in order to get the things we want. In 1970, for example, Americans had to work more than three times as many hours to earn enough to buy a TV set as they did in the late 1980s. Similarly, they had to work twice as long in 1970 to afford new clothing and 25 percent longer to earn a new car.[9] What's more, our homes are larger today (the median size of new privately owned single-family homes in the United States was 1,785 square feet in 1985, versus 1,595 square feet in 1980, and just 1,385 square feet in 1968), our entertainment options are wider, and our life expectancy is longer.

[8]Office of Technology Assessment (OTA), Congress of the United States, *Technology and the American Economic Transition: Choices for the Future* (Washington: Government Printing Office, 1988), 3.

[9]OTA, *Technology and the American Economic Transition: Choices for the Future*, 66.

So what is going on? How is it that we seem to have more resources at lower prices than ever before?

The answer, in a word, is Alchemy.

As we noted in Chapter 1, traditional economic theory views the world as containing a fixed—and hence essentially scarce—supply of physical resources. There is only so much coal, oil, iron, gold, water, arable land, and so forth to go around. According to this way of looking at things, the only way to increase your real wealth—whether "you" are an individual or a society—is at someone else's expense.

The Theory of Alchemy, in contrast, recognizes that physical resources are neither scarce nor even finite—not in an era in which we possess the know-how to "make computers from dirt," as the mathematician Mitchell Feigenbaum recently put it. What counts today is not the particular minerals we find buried in our backyard, but our growing ability to make more and better use of whatever does happen to be there.

This is the heart of the Theory of Alchemy: wealth is the product not just of physical resources but of physical resources *and technology.* And of the two, technology is by far the more important.

Mathematically, this profound truth can be expressed as a simple formula:

$$W = PT^n$$

In this expression, W stands for wealth, P for physical resources (that is, the traditional measures of wealth such as land, labor, minerals, water, and so on), T for technology, and n for the exponential effect of technological advances on themselves. (As we shall see, technology has a multiplier effect on itself as each new technological advance becomes the foundation for another advance.)

This simple formula has enormous implications—not just in terms of improving our understanding of the economic basis of our society, but as the key to developing more effective strategies for our individual lives as consumers, businesspeople, and citizens. What this tells us is that we no longer have to play the zero-sum game. Instead of finding better ways to slice up the same small pie, in the alchemic world we can find a way to bake a new and bigger pie.

For most of the past five or six thousand years, ever since the earliest days of organized society, people have thought of wealth as being an abundant supply of the physical necessities of life—namely, food, shelter, and clothing. In the earliest societies, the sources of these necessities were obvious: land, livestock, and building materials (which, depending on where you lived, could be anything from timber to mud to blocks of ice). The more of these physical resources you possessed, the wealthier you were considered to be.

Even in the most primitive societies, however, mere possession of physical resources was not in and of itself enough to guarantee anyone survival, much less comfort or luxury. You could own all the land and livestock in the world and still starve to death if you didn't know how to hunt and dress game, or sow and reap crops, or slaughter and butcher cattle. In order for your physical resources to do you any good, in other words, you needed to know how to make use of them; you needed some smattering of what today we might call basic technology.

It was this technology—this knowledge of how to make productive use of the raw materials of nature—that made resources like land, livestock, and building materials worth having in the first place. It was the discovery of fire—or at least the discovery of how to start and control fires—that made wood worth collecting. It was the invention of bread—which is to say, the development of milling and baking— that made grains like wheat and rye worth cultivating. It was the development of smelting that made ores like iron and tin worth mining.

In short, from the very beginnings of civilization technology was at least as important a component of wealth as physical resources. Indeed, of the two, technology has always been by far the more important, for without the appropriate technology physical resources are useless. To put it another way, it is technology that separates the wheat from the chaff.

Thus we arrive at the First Law of Alchemy:

By enabling us to make productive use of particular raw materials, technology determines what constitutes a physical resource.

Although this fact may seem obvious today, it was not evident throughout most of history. The reason is that until recently technology advanced quite slowly. Untold generations were born and died in the centuries it took for the Stone Age to give way to the Iron Age, for the Iron Age to give way to the Bronze Age. Modes of transportation, farming methods, medical practices, building techniques—for millennia, these and other technologies rarely changed noticeably within a single individual's lifetime. As a result, technology's impact on society was taken for granted to such an extent that it was as if it didn't exist. (Or, for those who did notice it, technology was treated, for decision-making purposes, as a constant over their lifetimes.)

To a South Sea islander in the late nineteenth century, for example, the fact that palm fronds could be woven in a certain way to make a roof for his hut seemed to be an integral part of the nature of palm fronds. Living as he did in a society in which hut roofs had been woven out of palm fronds for as long as anyone could remember, it would not occur to him that what made palm fronds a precious physical resource was a particular body of knowledge—namely, the technology of frond weaving. As far as he and his fellow South Sea islanders were concerned, palm fronds were by definition a building material—useful and hence valuable. Weaving them into roofs was as basic and natural a part of his life as, say, spearfishing.

To argue that palm fronds somehow did not constitute a valuable physical resource in their own right would make no more sense to our South Sea islander than to argue that fish were somehow not inherently valuable, either. How could they not be? Like palm fronds, fish always had been necessities of life, and always would be. It was obvious: the more you possessed, whether fish or palm fronds, the wealthier you were.

The fact is, of course, that just like palm fronds, fish *don't* constitute an inherently valuable resource. They represent food only to the society that possesses the technology of fishing. Without that technology, fish are nothing more than shadowy shapes that you might occasionally glimpse darting beneath the waves.

The crucial importance of technology becomes evident to us only when we see it shift massively in a relatively short time. For our South Sea islander, the arrival of a missionary with a supply of galvanized tin roofs would have likely done the trick. Faced with a different—and presumably better—way of building his hut, he might well have found himself reconsidering his view of palm fronds (along with the technology of frond weaving) and what they represented. Certainly, the palm fronds would have no longer represented wealth the way they used to. In this new situation, the wealthy man might be the one with the best relationship with the missionary.

It's only recently that technology has begun advancing quickly enough to catch our attention in this way. Again, consider oil, one of the staple resources of the modern era. Little more than a century or so ago petroleum was regarded as nothing more than a sticky black substance—"an odd, mysterious grease," it was called—that one occasionally came across seeping up through the rocks in out-of-the-way places. Even after Col. Edwin L. Drake drilled the world's first producing oil well in Titusville, Pennsylvania, in 1859, oil wasn't considered good for much beyond serving as a lubricant, a patent medicine, and a rather smoky and vile-smelling fuel for oil lamps. It wasn't until 1885, when Gottlieb Daimler and Carl Benz developed the first lightweight internal combustion engines that could burn a petroleum by-product known as gasoline—a by-product that up until then had been regarded as useless waste—that oil came to be considered a valuable resource.

By the early 1970s, of course, the petrochemical industry had grown into one of the world's largest, and oil—as both a fuel and a chemical feedstock—had become a linchpin of the global economy. What's more, as a direct result of the importance of oil, the barren desert kingdoms of the Persian Gulf, which happened to be located on top of one of the biggest petroleum deposits on earth, had gone from being among the world's poorest and least consequential countries to among its richest and most influential.

Indeed, in our lifetimes technology has exploded as never before. As Ralph Gomery, the longtime chief scientist of International Business Machines Corporation, recently noted: "When my father was young, he used to take a horse-drawn carriage to the railroad station. There were no automobiles, no telephones, no atomic bomb, no man on the moon. But by the time he died, he had flown in a jet and had seen all those other things happen. No generation had ever been through a transformation like that."[10]

We have seen, in other words, technology transform chaff into wheat and wheat into chaff before our very eyes. In recent years, we have watched technology make important resources of commodities as mundane and ubiquitous as sand (the raw material from which we make

[10]Gene Bylinsky, "Technology in the Year 2000," *Fortune*, 18 July 1988, 92–93.

silicon chips) and sea water (from which a variety of minerals ranging from gold to magnesium can be extracted). At the same time, we have seen it diminish—if not actually erase—the importance of such once key resources as natural rubber (replaced by synthetic rubber), tin (increasingly superseded by aluminum and plastics), aluminum (itself being supplanted by newly developed ceramics and carbon fiber composites), copper (demand for which is slowing as a result of recent advances in fiber-optics and superconductivity), and sheet steel (which is beginning to see competition from light, corrosion-resistant superpolymers).

The technology considered by the First Law of Alchemy—the technology that enables us to make use of particular raw materials and, in so doing, defines what constitutes a valuable physical resource—can be called *definitional technology*. Clearly, definitional technology plays an enormously important role—probably the most important role—in determining a society's wealth. But it is hardly the only kind of technology to affect us in this way. There is a second category of technology that we must consider—the technology that controls how much we have of an already defined physical resource.

Although we live in a constantly changing world—indeed, in a world in which the rate of change is constantly accelerating—not everything in our world changes every day. There is at any given moment an existing level of definitional technology—which is to say, an existing base of currently defined physical resources—that for all practical purposes we can and do consider to be the measure of what is available to us. In the 1980s, for example, our resource base consisted of such relatively familiar commodities such as bauxite, copper, coal, iron, gold, natural gas, petroleum, silicon, timber, tin, uranium, and so forth.

A hundred years ago that list would have looked very different (bauxite, silicon, and uranium would have been absent, for example, while ivory and whale oil might have been present). A decade from now it will be different again, no doubt in ways that we cannot today imagine. Nonetheless, one must work with the tools and resources one has at the time. In the 1980s, therefore, as at virtually every other moment in history, it made sense to ask the question: how can we increase our supply of what we currently regard as valuable physical resources?

Reading history, one might quite understandably come to the conclusion that the best way—indeed, the only way—to increase one's supply of physical resources is to take them from someone else. After all, not only have conventional economists regarded the struggle for prosperity as a zero-sum game, but most historians have also viewed the world in that light. Indeed, the notion that the resource pie was fixed and that a larger slice for you inevitably meant a smaller slice for me has always struck the vast majority of humanity as a matter of basic common sense. This notion, just like the Aristotelian notion that the sun revolves around the earth, seemed to accord with the evidence of our senses. What could be more obvious? If someone else had something, you could get it by taking it away from him.

In fact, however, the resource base has never been fixed—and not simply because the nature of its components are always changing as definitional technology advances. If the base were fixed, how could the worldwide reserves of oil, gas, copper, gold, silver, and the other commodities we cited earlier possibly have increased between the early 1970s and the late 1980s? The fact is, even in the context of a given set of previously defined physical resources, the supply of resources is always expanding.

It's not that vast new amounts of oil or gas or copper are somehow spontaneously being created deep in the bowels of the earth. The amount of these commodities is pretty much the same as it's always been less, of course, what we've consumed over the millennia. But the *amount* of a resource is not the same as the *supply* of a resource. The amount of a resource is how much of it physically exists in the universe. The supply of a resource is how much is known to exist and is physically available for our use—a figure that is determined as much by how we use it as by the quantity we happen to have available.

This leads us to the Second Law of Alchemy:

Technology determines our supply of existing physical resources by determining both the efficiency with which we use resources and our ability to find, obtain, distribute, and store them.

What makes a physical resource a resource—as opposed, say, to just a pretty rock or an annoying black goo—is its usefulness. Take oil, for example. One of the things that makes oil such a valuable physical resource is that we can refine it into gasoline and use it to power our cars. In this context, the most sensible way of measuring how much oil we have is not in terms of how many barrels it can fill up (filling up barrels, after all, isn't really what we want to do with the stuff), but in how many miles of driving we can get out of it.

The actual amount of oil buried in the earth (the number of barrels or gallons) is irrelevant. What counts is how much good the oil we know we have will do us—in other words, the supply.

Clearly, a veritable ocean of oil won't do us any good if we don't know it's there. Nor will it do us any good if we can find it but can't get to it. Nor if we can obtain it but can't move it to where we want it. Nor, finally, if we can distribute it to where we want it but can't find a way to store it there until we need it.

Beyond these constraints, there's the question of how we actually use it. If I've got a car that gets ten miles to the gallon and you've got a car that gets twenty miles to the gallon, the same amount of gasoline will get you twice as far as it will get me. In other words, even though we may both have the same number of gallons of gas, your effective supply is twice as big as mine.

From this it should be clear that there are basically two ways to increase the supply of a previously defined physical resource: (1) we can improve our ability to find, obtain, distribute, and store it; and (2) we can improve the efficiency with which we use it.

The first set of abilities constitutes what we might call *supply technology*. The second set can be labeled *use technology*. Together, they constitute the general category of technology considered by the Second Law of Alchemy—*quantity technology*, or technology that determines the available quantity of existing physical resources.

Of the two kinds of quantity technologies, the technology of supply has the more straightforward impact on our resource base. Consider its effect on the supply of oil and natural gas over the past two or three decades. To begin with, advances in geology (our ability to find oil and gas) led to the discovery in 1968 of the huge oil field beneath Prudhoe Bay on Alaska's North Slope—as a result of which estimates of total global oil reserves were revised upwards by nearly 10 billion barrels. On top of that, improvements in drilling techniques (our ability to obtain oil and gas) allowed gas producers who had previously never delved deeper than five or ten thousand feet to sink wells six miles or more into the earth's crust—thus giving them access to huge reservoirs they'd never before been able to tap. In addition, the evolution of the supertanker and the advance of pipeline construction methods (our ability to distribute oil and gas) enabled new discoveries to be brought on-stream almost as quickly as they could be made. And finally, the development of relatively safe above- and below-ground storage tanks gave us the ability to store heating oil in our homes and put a gas station on virtually every street corner.

In general, the four aspects of the technology of supply—the ability to find, obtain, distribute, and store a resource—constitute a kind of conceptual pipeline through which all physical resources must flow for them to be of any value to us. Our ability to clear up bottlenecks at any of those four points thus effectively increases our supply of a given resource.

In the case of oil and gas, the worst bottleneck we face as we enter the 1990s involves distribution. Over the past decade or two, we have become very good at finding, obtaining, and storing oil and gas. But as was illustrated by the horrendous *Exxon Valdez* spill that disfigured Alaska's Prince William Sound in 1989, our ability to transport oil safely still leaves much to be desired. As a result, we have (possibly with unconscious wisdom) let potentially huge supplies of oil and gas—such as the large, highly promising federal tracts in Alaska, off the California coast, and in the Gulf of Mexico—go unexplored.

This is true of most currently defined physical resources in the alchemic world. The biggest constraint on supply is not the difficulty of finding, obtaining, or storing resources, but the inability to distribute them efficiently to where they will do us the most good.

Perhaps nowhere has the frustration of this bottleneck been more glaringly illustrated than in famine-ravaged Ethiopia. As difficult as it may be to believe, Ethiopia was once considered the breadbasket of northern Africa. Even when the northern provinces of Eritrea and Tigre were stricken by drought in the early and mid-1980s, the country's main agricultural region—the south—continued to produce food in ample, if not abundant, quantities. Unfortunately, the lack of good roads and transportation facilities—not to mention a Marxist government that was attempting to put down an Eritrean-based insurrection—prevented supplies from getting to the north, where they were so badly needed.

In 1985, a massive international relief effort was undertaken to alleviate the famine in the north. As a result of appeals such as the hugely popular Live-Aid concerts, a veritable mountain of grain—more than 500,000 tons in all—was shipped to Ethiopia that year. For all the good intentions, however, very few hungry people got fed. What happened was that most of the grain wound up rotting in warehouses in the eastern Ethiopian port cities of Assab, Massawa, and Djibouti. As the relief workers discovered to their dismay, what Ethiopia needed wasn't more food, but more trucks and more roads.

Of course, advancing the technology of supply is not the only way to expand the base of currently defined physical resources. We can also grow the pie, as it were, by improving the efficiency with which we employ a particular resource—in other words, by advancing our level of use technology.

A classic example of how an advance in the technology of use can expand the resource base was the response of the automobile industry to the so-called fuel shortages of the early 1970s. By replacing $300 carburetors with $25 computerized fuel injectors, automakers doubled the fuel efficiency of new cars in less than a decade—in the process, improving the average fuel efficiency of all cars on the road by more than 35 percent (from an average of 13.5 miles per gallon in 1976 to better than 18.3 mpg in 1986).[11] In effect they increased the supply of gasoline by well over a third.

Similarly, by developing new and better insulation materials, construction techniques, and microelectronic control technologies, builders have vastly increased the efficiency with which people can heat and cool their homes. As a result, residential electricity use in the United States is expected to fall by 50 percent by the year 2005—in effect doubling the supply of energy resources that we use to generate electricity.[12]

As impressive as gains like these may seem, compared to the technology of supply, the technology of use has always been something of a neglected area. Before the fear of shortages gripped the world in the early 1970s, engineers and entrepreneurs generally felt that the easiest

[11]U.S. Department of Commerce, Bureau of the Census, *Statistical Abstract of the United States 1988* (Washington: Government Printing Office, 1988), 601.

[12]OTA, *Technology and the American Economic Transition*, 113.

way to increase the resource base was simply to get more of whatever it was they needed—to discover new oil deposits, to acquire or develop more arable land, and so on. The exception was during wartime, when artificially created shortages forced people to figure out ways of using what they had more efficiently. During World War II, for example, U.S. can manufacturers coped with government tin rationing by developing a new electrolytic plating process that cut their tin requirements by nearly two-thirds. But such lessons were generally forgotten when the war ended and access to the missing resources was restored.

The same seems true today. The main reason automakers are continuing to try to improve the fuel efficiency of their cars is not primarily because anyone is at least for the moment worried about the prospect of another round of gasoline shortages, but because of concerns about pollution (or, to look at it another way, because inefficient engines threaten to create a shortage of a resource that an increasing number of people consider to be even more precious than gasoline—namely, clean air). In any case, the fact is that as the fear of shortages recedes, so too does our incentive to develop more and more efficient methods of using our currently defined base of physical resources. As a result, the technology of use may never be fully exploited.

Still, even a temporary effort to improve use technology can yield enormous, lasting results. The advances in use technology that were spurred by the energy crisis of the 1970s—which, not so coincidentally, President Jimmy Carter called the "moral equivalent of war"—wound up improving overall global fuel efficiency by fully 20 percent in the 1980s. (That is, it cut worldwide energy consumption per unit of gross national product by one-fifth.) As a result, global oil demand declined by 7 percent between 1979 and 1987—this despite the fact that both population and industrial output were significantly higher in 1987 than they were in 1979.[13] (In the United States, the figures were even more dramatic: in the fifteen years following the 1973 oil crisis, America cut its oil use per dollar of GNP by one-third, as a result of which it managed to reduce its absolute oil consumption by 15 percent.)[14]

What's more, according to the International Energy Agency, even without any new technological breakthroughs—that is, simply by fully

[13]Cook, "We're Not Going to Freeze in the Dark," 107.

[14]Peter Nulty, "How to Keep OPEC on Its Back," *Fortune*, 26 May 1986, 88.

implementing the ones we've already made—global energy use per unit of GNP should drop an additional 30 percent by the year 2000.[15] In other words, solely as a result of the advances in the technology of use that were achieved in the decade of the 1980s, the world's effective supply of energy resources will be fully 50 percent larger in the year 2000 than it was in 1980.

In all, noted the U.S. Office of Technology Assessment in its ground-breaking 1988 report, *Technology and the American Economic Transition*, "optimal use of new technology could result in a forty to sixty percent decline in the [demand for] natural resources, even when there is rapid economic growth."[16] Cutting our need for resources by half, of course, has the effect of doubling our supply of them. Clearly, advances in use technology can have a stunning impact on the size of our resource base.

As the First and Second Laws of Alchemy indicate, our base of physical resources—and thus our wealth—is determined by the advance of technology. But then, we might ask, what controls the advance of technology?

This question brings us to the most important realization of all—that of the Third Law of Alchemy. This law explains what determines the advance of technology—and hence the nature of the key to increasing our wealth.

As we noted in Chapter 1, scientific and technological advance does not—indeed, cannot—occur in isolation. It depends on the ability of scientists and engineers to keep up with the latest developments, to cross-pollinate, to learn from the experience of others. As Sir Isaac Newton once put it, "If I have seen further it is by standing on the shoulders of giants."[17] Without access to the work of Nicolaus Copernicus, Galileo Galilei might never have known what to make of his observations of Jupiter's moons. Without knowledge of the pioneering

[15]Cook, "We're Not Going to Freeze in the Dark," 107.

[16]Office of Technology Assessment, *Technology and the American Economic Transition: Choices for the Future Summary*, (Washington: Government Printing Office, 1988), 52.

[17]In a letter to Robert Hooke, 5 February 1675/6, quoted in *The Concise Oxford Dictionary of Quotations*, new ed. (London: Oxford University Press, 1986), 176.

field equations of the brilliant nineteenth-century Scottish physicist James Clerk Maxwell, the twentieth-century Italian engineer Guglielmo Marconi would not have been able to invent the radio—nor German-born Albert Einstein develop his theory of relativity.

In short, the speed at which technology advances depends on how easily members of a society can access and share their acquired knowledge—that is, it depends on the level of *information-processing technology*.

Thus we arrive at the Third Law of Alchemy:

The rate at which a society's technology advances is determined by the relative level of its ability to process information.

Though this has always been the case, never has this basic truth been more apparent than in the last few decades. Ours, after all, is an era that believes in the absolute value of information, that subscribes to the notion that "information is power," and that even occasionally refers to itself as the Information Age. Indeed, by the late 1980s, the processing, communication, or manipulation of information was the principal occupation of one out of every four U.S. workers—one out of every three, if you counted teachers and others employed in the education sector. Similarly, as the century's final decade began, well over 40 percent of all new U.S. investment in plant and equipment was in the category of information technology (things like computers, photocopiers, fax machines, and the like)—more than double the share ten years earlier.[18]

Former U.S. Treasury Secretary W. Michael Blumenthal summed it up well in a 1988 article entitled "The World Economy and Technological Change." Information, he wrote, has come to be regarded as "the key to modern economic activity—a basic resource as important today as capital, land and labor have been in the past."[19]

As resources go, we certainly seem to have an ample supply of information. But appearances can be deceiving. Clearly, the amount of

[18]OTA, *Technology and the American Economic Transition: Choices for the Future*, 17.

[19]W. Michael Blumenthal, "The World Economy and Technological Change," *Foreign Affairs* 66, no.3 (1988), 534.

information we have is growing every day, at a faster and faster rate. Indeed, it has been estimated that we have added more to the sum total of human knowledge in the last century than in the entire previous history of mankind put together. But, as is the case with other resources, finding or developing new information is only part of the battle. After all, what is the point of discovering some new fact about the universe, whether it happens to be a fundamental law of nature or a new improved way to manufacture chewing gum, if no one who can make use of the information ever receives it?

As with any resource, information is useful to us only to the extent that we can get it to where it is needed. Thus it is, as Blumenthal has noted, that "a country's comparative advantage lies in its ability to utilize effectively the new information [-processing] technology."[20]

Viewed in alchemic terms, the critical importance of information-processing technology is obvious. If information is the most important resource we have (because it is the raw material on which technological advance depends), then the quantity technology of information—namely, information-processing technology—must be the most important technology we have (because it determines the usable supply of information).

Humanity's first big breakthrough in information-processing technology was the invention and development of writing some five or six thousand years ago. Before the invention of writing, ideas and information could be passed on only verbally. Among other things, that meant that unless you happened to meet up personally with the particular individual who had originated some new concept or discovery, your knowledge of his work was bound to be at best second-hand and, thus, potentially inaccurate. (After all, in a pre-literate society, there are no original sources to look up—except the originator himself.) Although humanity's oral tradition is certainly a rich one—over the millennia it has managed to pass on everything from the invention of the wheel to the epic poetry of Homer—verbal communication has never been very good at disseminating information quickly, widely, and accurately.

The invention of writing was thus an essential fundament of the economic basis of early civilization. Indeed, though today we may think of writing mainly in terms of personal and artistic expression, the fact

[20]Blumenthal, "The World Economy and Technological Change," 537.

is that most of the earliest examples of writing we have, such as the clay tablets on which are etched the cuneiform script of the ancient Sumerians and Babylonians, are either business receipts, government records, or explanations of agricultural techniques.

The next major step forward in humanity's ability to process information came in the Middle Ages—a mere six hundred or so years ago—with Gutenberg's invention of the printing press.[21] Before Gutenberg, the only way to reproduce written material was to have it copied by hand—an expensive and time-consuming process that severely limited the size of the audience to whom a writer could pass on knowledge. The reliance on hand copying also limited the accuracy with which knowledge could be transmitted, for as texts were copied and recopied, errors were bound to creep in. The printing press, of course, changed all that. In effect, it introduced both mass production and standardization to information processing—advances that paved the way for the industrial revolution.

In our century, we have seen the third major advance in information processing: the development of the computer, by far the most significant invention of the modern era.

For the most part, we tend to think of computers in terms of their speed. As Blumenthal has noted, "In the seventeenth century, it took Johannes Kepler four years to calculate the orbit of Mars. Today a microprocessor can do it in four seconds flat."[22] That is no mere parlor trick. But what makes the computer special is more than just its ability to perform lightning-fast calculations. As tremendously valuable as it is, that ability alone would be as much a curse as a blessing, accelerating the advance of knowledge, to be sure, but at the same time leaving us drowning in a flood of new information.

It is what the computer with human supervision can do with the results of its calculations that makes it such a profoundly significant innovation—its ability to sort through and collate data, its ability to link different sectors of society through complex communications networks, its ability to manage the transmission of information through those networks to wherever in the world it is needed.

[21]While printing originally began in eighth-century China, it was Gutenberg's printing press and method of using moveable type that made it widely available.

[22]Blumenthal, "The World Economy and Technological Change," 534.

As a result of these abilities, the widespread integration of computers in modern society has not only ignited an information explosion but also has given us the means to manage the overwhelming fallout of that explosion. The fact remains, however, that we are still better at producing new information than we are at accessing and sharing it. Indeed, technology is advancing so rapidly on so many fronts that the main constraint on innovation today is not so much the capacity of engineers and entrepreneurs to come up with new ideas, but their ability to keep abreast of and integrate the latest developments from fields outside their own particular specialty.

This, then, is the way to increase the size of the pie. The more we can improve our ability to process information, the faster technology in general will advance. The faster technology in general advances, the greater its ability both to increase the effective supply of existing physical resources and to define entirely new ones—and the richer we will be.

What, in practical terms, does it mean to say that as a result of modern technology we effectively have access to an unlimited supply of resources? To begin with, it means that the accumulation of resources is no longer the key to achieving wealth.

That certainly was the lesson learned by the various cartels that attempted to take advantage of the fear of resource scarcity that gripped the world in the early and mid-1970s. Between 1974 and 1975, no fewer than eight new cartels came into being, most of them agglomerations of Third World commodity exporters who believed they could dictate the price and supply of basic goods as diverse as bananas, bauxite, copper, rubber, timber, and tungsten. In 1978, there was even an attempt to set up an umbrella organization of cartels to coordinate the price-fixing efforts of the individual groups.

By the mid-1980s, every one of these cartels had for all practical purposes been driven out of business. So too had OPEC, once the *bête noire* of the industrialized world and the model for the other commodity cartels.

The flaw in the cartels' logic was the assumption that the industrialized nations could not survive without the cartels' commodities, that consumers would pay any price rather than have their supplies interrupted.

41

In fact, as prices rose, customers began looking around for substitutes—substitutes that technology gave them the means to find. For example, when the tin cartel artificially pushed up the price of tin to a record $12,000 a ton in the early 1980s, users wound up making a massive switch to aluminum, glass, cardboard, and plastics. Back in 1972, 80 percent of all U.S. beverage cans had been made of tin plate; by 1985, virtually all U.S. beer cans and 87 percent of soft-drink cans were aluminum. In all, as a result of the tin producers' greed, worldwide tin consumption fell by 15 percent between 1980 and 1985.[23]

Similarly, as the price of copper rose throughout the 1970s, the telecommunications industry began to accelerate the development of new technologies such as fiber-optics that didn't depend on copper wiring and cable. As a result, by the end of the 1980s, U.S. telephone companies had installed upwards of 1.5 million miles of fiber-optic cable, and at least two of the regional Bell operating companies had announced plans to completely replace their copper cable with all-fiber networks within the next twenty years.[24]

There is a basic lesson to be learned from this: namely, *in the alchemic world, the market has no corners.*

While the old-fashioned economist attempts to succeed by cornering the market in some valuable commodity, the Alchemist recognizes that commercial enterprises based on the exploitation of scarcity are doomed.

When it comes to assessing the value of commodities, the Alchemist is a true fundamentalist. He knows that in a world of effectively unlimited resources, because there are few if any resources for which one cannot find substitutes, a particular commodity is not worth just what the market happens to be willing to pay for it. True, the price set by the market is the classic economic definition of value. But ours is no longer a classic world. In the alchemic world, the market price reflects merely a commodity's speculative value. The Alchemist's concern, by contrast, is with the commodity's *fundamental productive value*—its price relative to the price of other commodities that can be used to fill the same need. Any price above that level is not worth paying.

[23]Kenneth R. Sheets, "Cartels Choke on Gluts of Raw Material," *U.S. News & World Report,* 25 November 1985, 62–63.

[24]U.S. Department of Commerce, *1989 U.S. Industrial Outlook,* 30th annual ed. (Washington: Government Printing Office, 1989), 26–27.

The fundamental productive value of a commodity is analogous to the book value of a company. The book value of a company is based not on the stock market's partly analytic, partly emotional sense of what a company is worth, but on a strict accounting of the cash that the company's assets could fetch if they were sold off separately. In the 1980s a new generation of Wall Street raiders transformed the corporate landscape—and made themselves fortunes in the process—by breaking up (or threatening to break up) companies whose market value was less than their fundamental book value. So, too, in the 1990s and beyond, will Alchemists transform the resource landscape as they increasingly focus on the fundamental productive value of commodities.

For example, suppose a specific application in, say, dentistry utilizes one ounce of gold. And suppose a synthetic material is developed that can do the same job at a cost of $250. Although gold might be trading on the open market at $400 an ounce, an Alchemist would consider its productive value for this application to be only $250 an ounce. If there were no other applications for gold, the Alchemist would expect its price eventually to fall to this fundamental level. However, since there are usually many applications for a specific commodity, the fundamental productive value is usually an average of several different fundamental values for these different uses.

Similarly, suppose you needed to burn 400 gallons of heating oil in order to heat your home for a year. If the price of heating oil happened to be $1 a gallon, your annual heating bill would be $400. But how would you reckon the productive value of the heating oil? That would depend on the price of alternatives. Say that a year's worth of heat from natural gas would cost you $500. In that case, the Alchemist would consider the true productive value of the oil to be $1.25 a gallon, and would expect its price eventually to rise to that fundamental level (subject, of course, to any changes in the price of natural gas and, more important, to any changes in the technologies relating to the available quantity of both fuels).

When it comes to resources, the Alchemist never forgets that this is a buyer's market, that as a result of technology, there is virtually no raw material for which one cannot find a substitute. No particular raw material is all that important in the overall scheme of things, and the real price of any raw material is determined as much by the price and supply of potential substitutes as by its own availability.

If accumulating resources is no longer the key to achieving wealth in the modern world, what is? In the 1960s, the movie *The Graduate* offered a one-word answer to that question: "plastics." In the 1990s, we offer a different (though no less pithy) answer: "distribution."

These days, as a result of the impact of advancing technology on the costs of labor and raw materials, the actual consumer cost of virtually every manufactured item has fallen. Most of this reduction in price has come because the actual production cost of an item has fallen to where it typically represents less than 20 percent of the retail price. By the late 1980s, for example, the actual cost of raw farm products and farm labor had come to represent less than 15 percent of the price grocery stores and restaurants charged customers for food. Similarly, only about 17 percent of the price of finished apparel was attributable to the actual cost of cloth and the labor needed to cut and sew it into shape.[25]

Most of the remaining 80 percent represents the cost of distribution. The reason distribution has come to represent such an outsized proportion of the consumer's price is that distribution cost has not declined as fast as production cost. This cost-reduction disparity reflects the fact that, with very few exceptions, we have yet to apply to our distribution networks the technological advances that have so profoundly transformed the rest of the supply pipeline.

It's not that we lack the know-how. Indeed, in many cases, the appropriate technology has been around for quite some time. America's food distributors, for example, could quickly improve their productivity by as much as 50 percent simply by taking widespread advantage of such already existing technological innovations as automatic handling equipment. Similarly, U.S. apparel manufacturers could cut their massive inventory costs in half by implementing the well-established "Quick Response" control system.

The point is that on the supply side of the alchemic equation, improvements in distribution have the potential to yield far greater savings than improvements in any other area. Suppose you run a company that produces a finished product that sells for $100. By our reckoning, $20 of that final price will represent your manufacturing costs (that is, the cost of labor and materials), while the remaining $80 will reflect the cost of distribution. A 20 percent cut in manufacturing

[25]OTA, *Technology and the American Economic Transition: Choices for the Future*, 207, 237.

costs—achieved, say, by moving your factory to the Far East—would therefore wind up reducing the final price of your finished product by $4. A 20 percent cut in distribution costs, by contrast, would shave $16 off the final price. In other words, the same increase in efficiency would produce four times the savings in distribution as it would in manufacturing.

In fact, the differential is bound to be even greater, for moving your factory to the Far East would inevitably increase your distribution costs, perhaps to the point where they wound up entirely offsetting whatever the manufacturing savings you'd manage to achieve. This is why the lion's share of Sony television sets and Nissan automobiles purchased by U.S. consumers are now assembled in the United States, as opposed to some lower-cost labor market.

The emphasis on distribution represents a significant change in the nature of economic opportunity. Until well into the twentieth century, most of the greatest personal fortunes in American history—fortunes like those of the Astors (fur trading), the Rockefellers (oil), the Carnegies (steel), and the Fords (automobiles)—were built on the bedrock of natural resources and manufacturing.

In our modern alchemic world, however, the route to wealth has shifted. In the last decade or two, the biggest personal fortunes have all been earned by individuals like Fred Smith (who founded Federal Express) and H. Ross Perot (Electronic Data Systems)—proto-Alchemists who made their mark by coming up with new and better ways to move goods and share information.

Perhaps the best example of this sort of proto-Alchemist is that of Sam Walton. Though not nearly as well known as many other tycoons, Walton had by the late 1980s become the richest man in America— the result of his intuitive alchemic understanding of the importance of technology and the unrealized potential in distribution.

The son of a Midwestern farm-mortgage banker, Walton began his business life in 1940, at the age of twenty-one, as a trainee with J. C. Penney. After serving in the army in World War II, he moved to Arkansas and opened a small five-and-dime store.

A few years later, as Penney and the other national retailers began opening discount stores in metropolitan areas, Walton got the idea of introducing the same kind of service to rural America. Unable to interest any of the established chains in backing him, Walton eventually decided to go it alone. In 1962, he opened his first Wal-Mart store in tiny Rogers, Arkansas.

Wal-Mart was hardly an overnight success. The problem was that discounters depended on distributors to supply them with merchandise, and as Walton later told a magazine interviewer, "We didn't have distributors falling over themselves to service us like our competitors did in larger towns."[26] Indeed, in the early days of discounting, there simply weren't any distributors willing to service many of the small towns in which Wal-Mart wanted to do business.

So what Walton did was start his own distribution system. As he put it, "Our only alternative was to build our own warehouse so we could buy in volume at attractive prices and store the merchandise."[27]

But Walton didn't build just any distribution system. He realized that the key to success lay not just in his ability to get goods to his stores, but in being able to keep track of what was selling and what wasn't—that is, in moving the goods *and* sharing the information. Walton took advantage of the latest advances in data processing and communications technology to construct the most sophisticated automated distribution system the world had ever seen. Today, his growing network of stores and mammoth distribution centers are equipped with the latest automated materials-handling equipment as well as state-of-the-art laser scanning devices that automatically monitor inventory levels. What's more, the stores and the distribution centers are connected by a six-channel satellite computer-communication system worthy of the Pentagon; it allows orders and merchandising information to be passed back and forth at the speed of light.

As a result of this emphasis on distribution, Wal-Mart has grown into a $30 billion-a-year behemoth that sometime early in the 1990s will probably pass Sears and K-Mart on its way to becoming the largest retail chain in the world. And though he still drove a battered old Ford pickup truck with cages in the back for his two favorite bird dogs, by 1989 Sam Walton was worth more than Donald Trump, Rupert Murdoch, and the late Malcolm Forbes put together—his alchemic understanding of technology and distribution having earned him and his family a personal fortune of something on the order of $9 billion.

[26]Howard Rudnitsky, "Play it Again, Sam," *Forbes*, 10 August 1987, 48.

[27]Rudnitsky, "Play it Again, Sam," 48.

DEMAND-SIDE ALCHEMY

In which we define the Fourth Law of Alchemy, which explains how technology determines the nature of demand; the Fifth Law of Alchemy, which explains how technology determines the aggregate level of demand; and, most important of all, how virtually the whole of our modern economy is built upon the alchemic demand that these two laws explain.

"MONEY," observed the Elizabethan philosopher Francis Bacon, "is like muck, not good except it be spread."[1] Economists and Alchemists alike would have to agree. Except to the pathological miser, the accumulation of money is not an end in itself. Although we may equate it with comfort, security, and power, money is merely a medium through which we can acquire the specific things and create the particular conditions we happen to need or want. The point of money, in other words, is to be spent.

What is true of money in particular is also true of wealth in general. Whether we define wealth in terms of units of currency or supplies of resources, what makes it worth having is the ability it gives us to live the kind of life we desire. Although this may seem obvious, it is worth noting because too often we rate the economic well-being of a society solely in terms of its productive capacity—that is, the amount of wealth

[1]Francis Bacon, "Of Seditions and Troubles," *Essays,* quoted in *The Concise Oxford Dictionary of Quotations,* new ed. (London: Oxford University Press, 1986), 13.

of one sort or another that it can produce. We forget that output is meaningless unless it can be transformed into useful input, that supply does us no good unless it can be matched with some corresponding demand. As Keynes noted, "Consumption . . . is the sole end of all economic activity."[2]

Of course, if the only point of supply is to satisfy demand, then there would seem to be no point in having more resources than we can actually use. And, in fact, there isn't. Indeed, in conventional economic terms, an overabundance of resources is just as bad (if not actually worse) than an insufficiency of them. As attractive as the prospect of unlimited resources may seem to be, we thus must ask ourselves whether the alchemic power of technology to provide unlimited physical resources might actually be more of a curse than a blessing.

The "problem" of too much wealth has been a major concern of modern economists—in particular, Keynes, who worried that prosperity might actually wind up reducing demand. Specifically, Keynes believed that the richer people became, the smaller the proportion of their incomes they would spend.[3] The reason for this, Keynes said, was that when it came to spending or consuming, the average man was far more strongly motivated to satisfy "the immediate primary needs of [himself] and his family"—that is, to buy himself and his dependents food, clothing, and shelter—than to purchase whatever nonessentials he might be able to afford after these basic requirements had been met. "When a margin of comfort has been attained," Keynes insisted, the average person would be more likely to save than spend.[4]

At a time when Americans are regularly criticized by economists for not saving enough, Keynes' fear that affluence would swell savings at the expense of spending may seem puzzling if not actually perverse. In fact, it was—and still is—a perfectly legitimate concern. While a certain amount of thrift is essential to a society's economic well-being, if

[2]John Maynard Keynes, *The General Theory of Employment, Interest, and Money,* First Harvest/HBJ ed. (San Diego: Harcourt Brace Jovanovich, 1964), 104.

[3]"The fundamental psychological law upon which we are entitled to depend with great confidence . . . is that men are disposed, as a rule and on the average, to increase their consumption as their income increases, but not by as much as the increase in their income." Keynes, *The General Theory of Employment, Interest, and Money,* 96.

[4]Keynes, *The General Theory of Unemployment, Interest, and Money,* 97.

consumption does not keep pace with rising income and too much money winds up sitting in the bank unspent, prices will fall, jobs will be lost, and economic growth will grind to a halt.

Americans used to be enthusiastic if not actually excessive savers. Between 1865 and 1900, the total savings of Americans—in particular, the immigrants who swelled the nation's population during that period—increased nearly ninefold, from a total of $243 million in some 981,000 separate accounts to more than $2.1 billion in 5.4 million accounts. As remarkable as this growth may seem, total U.S. savings deposits grew even more rapidly over the next thirty years, by 1930 swelling to more than $28 billion in nearly 53 million accounts.[5]

The reasons for this astounding savings binge had more to do with the nature of the savers themselves than with any behavioral changes of the sort predicted by Keynes. By definition, the early immigrant had to be an enthusiastic saver; otherwise, he never would have been able to become an immigrant in the first place. For one thing, he had to have developed disciplined saving habits in his native land in order to have amassed the money required to buy passage to America. Then, once he arrived in America, he had to continue his unusual pattern of working and saving in order to be able to bring his family over. And even after he had accomplished that, he tended to continue saving—perhaps because, as Charles Dickens noted in 1864, "If you begin [saving] and go on with it for a little time, you come to have a sort of passion for it."[6]

In any case, rather than stifling growth, the impressive accumulation of savings in late nineteenth- and early twentieth-century America was a boon to development. The reason was that the expansive nature of the burgeoning U.S. economy in that period ensured that the demand for funds kept pace with the supply. Economically immature and relatively undeveloped, turn-of-the-century America was in the throes of rapid industrialization, and its appetite for the new goods and services made possible by recent technological advances was enormous. As a result, it eagerly lapped up the seemingly unlimited internal funds

[5]U.S. Department of Commerce, Bureau of the Census, *Statistical Abstract of the United States 1940* (Washington: Government Printing Office, 1941), 267.

[6]Charles Dickens, "My Account with Her Majesty," *All the Year Round Magazine,* 5 March 1864, 79–83.

generated by the seemingly unlimited thrift of immigrants. Indeed, it was immigrants' savings that ultimately provided the money to build the railroads, harbors, utility networks, and sanitation systems that were needed to transform the nation's vast economic potential into reality.[7]

Immigration tailed off sharply after World War I—dropping in the postwar decade to a third of what it had been in the prewar decade— the result of new immigration laws and restrictive quotas.[8] Nonetheless, the U.S. economy continued to expand through the 1920s, as did the level of savings. Of course, the nature of that expansion was now quite different. What made the 1920s roar from an economic point of view wasn't primarily what one might call fundamental growth—that is, the continuing construction of a productive infrastructure—but rather a frenzy of speculation as the demand for real goods exceeded the society's technological capacity to supply them. Although technological advances did cause real output to rise, the increase in production was insufficient to feed the newly acquired (if highly leveraged) fortunes that drove prices up far beyond anything that rationality or real value could justify. Whatever the reason, for a brief period America was giddy with unprecedented prosperity. The nation was on a binge as banks and corporations found themselves awash in money, much of which went into the stock market, fueling a boom that seemed to have no end.

Between the spring of 1926 and the spring of 1929, the Dow Jones Industrial Average more than doubled. It was the sort of growth that couldn't last, and of course it didn't. By the autumn of 1929, with interest rates high and economic growth slowing, what had become by then not so much a house but more a skyscraper of cards began to collapse. The resulting crash took a good proportion of the nation's financial structures and institutions down with it—including nearly half the nation's banks.[9] Overnight, millions of people saw their life savings wiped out. Those whose savings weren't completely buried

[7]Paul Zane Pilzer with Robert Deitz, *Other People's Money* (New York: Simon and Schuster, 1989), 25.

[8] *Statistical Abstract of the United States 1989*, 9.

[9]Between 1929 and 1933, the number of banks of all kinds in the United States fell by more than 42 percent, from 25,330 to 14,624. *Statistical Abstract of the United States 1940*, 256.

under the rubble pulled whatever they could salvage out of the surviving banks (which, of course, made the survival of these institutions even more uncertain) and almost literally hid it under the mattress. As people withdrew their funds from circulation, the nation's money supply contracted, people stopped spending, and economic growth sputtered and died.

By the early 1930s, America—along with most of the rest of the world—was mired in a massive depression. It was from this vantage point that Keynes developed his landmark theory of oversaving. As vital as individual thrift had been to the development of the world's industrialized economies, Keynes realized, what was needed now to get things moving again wasn't saving but spending. This realization marked a major departure in economic thought. For most of history, people had considered the biggest economic challenge to be that of supply: how to provide themselves with sufficient amounts of food, clothing, shelter, and the other necessities of life. As Keynes saw it, however, this was no longer the case. The biggest challenge faced by modern economies, he argued, was that of demand—specifically, the problem of how to sustain it.

Clearly, an insufficiency of demand was at the root of the continuing depression of the 1930s. But even looking beyond the immediate crisis to the day when everyone would have everything they needed—a comfortable house, indoor plumbing, a car, warm clothing—Keynes saw serious trouble. For the more people had, he reasoned, the less they would need. And the less they needed, the less they would spend.

Keynes did more than simply analyze what he regarded as the self-destructive tendencies of modern economies. He lobbied vigorously for governments to adopt a series of activist policies designed to stimulate demand—among them deficit spending, progressive taxation, and the manipulation of interest rates—for Keynes was convinced that without such measures doom was inevitable. As he saw it, unless governments in effect forced people to keep spending as they got more of what they needed, the economy would eventually and inevitably implode again, a victim, as it were, of its own success.

Over the next several decades, however, a strange thing happened. Although Keynes' views eventually became the conventional wisdom among both economists and government policymakers, his proposed solutions were never completely adopted. Yet the Great Depression ended, people began to get everything they needed—*and then more of everything they needed, and then even more of everything they needed*—and still the economy didn't implode.

More than fifty years after Keynes first issued his dire warnings—and a quarter-century after Milton Friedman declared on behalf of the entire economic establishment that "we are all Keynesians now" (a sentiment later echoed by President Richard Nixon)—one thing is clear. For all the elegance of his argument, Keynes was wrong. Increasing affluence has not stifled demand. Rather, consumer demand has so doggedly kept pace with rising incomes that it sometimes seems as if the two are joined at the hip. In the United States, for example, real per capita disposable personal income climbed by 174 percent between 1940 and 1987; in the same period, real per capita personal consumption spending rose by a nearly identical 172 percent.[10]

As a result, rather than imploding, our economy has continued to expand with a consistency that is almost frightening. To be sure, there have been some bad patches (a few of them quite severe). But, overall, economic growth has been marching steadily upward for the past half-century or so at an astonishing pace. Indeed, from Keynes' day right up to our own, America's wealth (as measured by its annual gross national product) has nearly quintupled in real terms.[11] If anything has imploded, it has been the credibility of conventional economics, which over the years has proved itself continually unable to explain the economic boom that persists to this day.

It is said that we can learn more from the errors of great thinkers than from the accuracies of ordinary minds. And Keynes was very much a great thinker. In this sense, it may be useful to consider just where he went wrong in his assumptions about demand.

Keynes was a pivotal figure in the history of economic thought, at the same time the last of the old breed and the first of the new—as Peter Drucker put it, "at once the legitimate heir and the liquidator of Adam Smith."[12] His legacy is thus somewhat contradictory, looking

[10]*Statistical Abstract of the United States 1989*, 424.

[11]In constant 1982 dollars, U.S. GNP rose from just under $773 billion in 1940 to nearly $3.9 trillion in 1987. From *Statistical Abstract of the United States 1989*, 421.

[12]Peter F. Drucker, "Keynes: Economics as a Magical System," *Virginia Quarterly Review*, 22 (Winter 1946), 532.

back to the past even as it anticipates the future, studded with modern insights that founder on antique attitudes.

Among Keynes' major contributions was the notion that demand had as much to do with subjective consumer psychology as with objective economic reality, that factors such as envy and self-esteem were every bit as significant in determining consumer spending habits as income and inflation.[13] Before Keynes, few economists bothered to wonder about the human sources of demand. All that mattered was that people needed things. How or why they might have come to conceive a particular need was considered irrelevant.

But for all his modern awareness of the psychological component of demand, when it came to the nature of human needs, Keynes—and the whole of mainstream economics that followed him—was very much rooted in the nineteenth century. Certainly, Keynes was right in assuming that consumer demand depended on the extent to which people had unsatisfied needs. But he was wrong in thinking that people's needs were basically fixed and absolute—that they were capable of eventually being met, at which point demand would be satiated.

This is the essence of the alchemic view of demand. In contrast to the conventional economist, with his tacit assumption that at their most basic level human needs mirror the essentially unvarying requirements of human physiology, the Alchemist recognizes that people's needs are neither fixed nor absolute. Rather, they are being redefined constantly. And what determines both the nature and pace of that redefinition is technology. This is what Keynes and virtually every other mainstream economist failed to recognize: that from the very beginnings of civilization, both the nature and degree of human need in any society—and hence the nature and degree of aggregate consumer demand—has always depended entirely on the level of that society's technology. Thus it is in our era of exponentially advancing technology that consumer demand has not diminished but rather has continued to expand.

The way in which technology defines human need—and hence determines the nature of consumer demand—is quite straightforward. By

[13]"[Human needs] fall into two classes—those needs which are absolute in the sense that we feel them whatever the situation of our fellow human beings may be, and those which are relative only in that their satisfaction lifts us above, makes us feel superior to, our fellows." J. M. Keynes, "Economic Possibilities for Our Grandchildren," *Essays in Persuasion* (London: Macmillan, 1931), 365–66.

providing us with new products or processes, advancing technology invariably induces changes in our basic behavior—changes that are sometimes so fundamental that before very long we cannot imagine living any other way. The new product or process on which our new way of living depends thus becomes essential to maintaining our way of life. In other words, it assumes the status of a necessity—something that we need in order to live the way we want.

The classic example of this sort of self-justifying innovation is the automobile. When it was first introduced, the automobile was considered to be a luxury—an expensive toy that men of means bought mainly to take their families for Sunday drives in the country. Over time, however, and not very much time at that, as mass production made car ownership practical for an increasingly wide public, people's notions of distance and mobility changed profoundly. Before long, a sizable chunk of the population had actually *moved* to the country—or at least to that convenient strip of it that we now call suburbia—and suddenly the car was a necessity. Indeed, for most suburban families, *two* cars were essential.

The introduction of the modern-style washing machine in the early 1920s provides an equally dramatic example of how technology determines what constitutes a need. Before the invention of the washing machine, doing the laundry was perhaps the single most onerous of all household chores—so onerous, in fact, that people simply didn't wash their clothes all that often; while they might hang them and brush them between wearings, it simply was not practical to launder them terribly frequently. As a result, most clothing was constructed to require a minimum of laundering. Shirts, for example, came with detachable collars and cuffs, the parts of the garment that got dirty most quickly.

To our modern eyes (and noses), the personal hygiene of our great-grandparents would thus have seemed intolerably grubby. (We, of course, would no doubt have struck them as absurdly fastidious.) What accounts for the difference in standards, of course, is a change in technology—specifically, the invention in 1922 of the electrically powered, agitator-type washer by Howard Snyder of Newton, Iowa.[14] Suddenly, laundry was no longer such a chore.

[14]The first electrically powered washing machine was actually invented in 1910 by Alva J. Fisher, and several models were on the market before World War I. But Snyder's agitator washer was the first to gain a sizable market.

In the early days, of course, a washing machine was hardly essential. After all, what ordinary working man needed to wear a clean shirt every day? The answer, of course, was that no one really *needed* to. Still, as long as it was possible, why not? Within a few years, wearing freshly laundered clothes was no longer an affectation solely of those wealthy enough to afford servants; to the contrary, it had become a staple of middle-class decency. By the mid-1930s, the detachable collar had gone the way of the horse and buggy (that is, completely and irrevocably out of fashion), and the washing machine was well on its way to becoming a necessity.

This process is a continual one; it doesn't just happen at the time a new technology is first introduced. Consider what happened with telephone usage in the 1980s. By 1980, the telephone was as integrated into the daily lives of Americans as any technological innovation in history. After more than half a century of exposure to it, people knew what it was, what it could do, and how they liked to use it. From a conventional economic point of view, therefore, one would have thought that the demand for telephone use was mature—that is, that it would be unlikely to expand much faster than the rate of general population growth. Yet over the next seven years, a period during which the U.S. population grew by 7 percent, the time Americans spent on the phone jumped by more than 24 percent.[15]

What created this unexpected new demand was the impact of advancing technology. Developments in cordless and cellular technology allowed phones to become so ubiquitous—by the late 1980s they were as likely to be found in cars, planes, and at poolside as on the kitchen wall or the bedroom night table—that it became virtually impossible to conceive of a situation in which anyone would have to stifle the impulse to make a call because a handset was not within easy reach. And not only were phones more convenient, but as a result of such technological innovations as call waiting and automatic redialing, telephones were also easier to use than ever.

In short, by providing consumers with a series of alternatives that hadn't before occurred to them, technology created a need that previously hadn't existed. There was no demand to speak of for a waterproof

[15]Trish Hall, "With Phones Everywhere, Everyone Is Talking More," *New York Times*, 11 October 1989, A-1.

portable telephone that one could take swimming—until, that is, telephone manufacturers developed such a device. Then, suddenly, every homeowner with a backyard pool had to have one.

So it is that by creating new products that soon become the basis of an entirely new way of life, technology creates needs that did not exist before (or at least were not perceived before).[16] Those new needs then proceed to generate consumer demand in a self-fulfilling cycle that is bound to continue as long as technology continues to advance.

We can state this formally as the Fourth Law of Alchemy:

> *By providing us with new products and processes that change the way in which we live, technology determines what constitutes a need, and hence the nature of consumer demand.*

Technology's role on the demand side of the alchemic equation is entirely analogous to its role on the supply side. In both cases, it is the definitive factor. Just as a society's level of technology at any given moment determines what particular raw materials will have value as resources to that society's producers, so too does its level of technology determine what sort of goods and services are likely to be in demand by its consumers.

The first step on the road to what we might call alchemic demand was taken some ten thousand years ago when the dominant form of human social organization began to shift from mainly nomadic tribes of hunter-gatherers to more stable agrarian communities. The change, of course, was prompted by advancing technology, namely the development of agriculture, which gave people for the first time a measure of control over their food supply. As a result, people could start planning for the future in a meaningful way. What's more, as people learned to cultivate crops and livestock more efficiently; they no longer had to spend virtually every waking hour making sure they would have enough to eat. For the first time, they could turn their attention to things other than mere survival.

One can legitimately call this the dawn of the age of alchemic demand, for it was then—as a result of technology—that the demand

[16]Depending on your philosophy, this may amount to the same thing.

for goods began to extend beyond what Keynes would have referred to as "immediate primary needs." (As Galbraith has observed, "Once a society has provided itself with food, clothing, and shelter . . . its members begin to desire other things."[17])

But this dawn did not quickly ripen into midday, or even morning. While humankind had moved beyond the margins of subsistence, it did not move very far for a very long time. As Keynes noted, "From the earliest times of which we have record—back, say, to two thousand years before Christ—down to the beginning of the eighteenth century, there was no very great change in the standard of living of the average man living in the civilized centers of the earth. Ups and downs certainly. Visitations of plague, famine and war. Golden intervals. But no progressive violent change."[18]

What happened in the eighteenth century to get things moving was another major advance in technology, namely the beginning of the industrial revolution. As the factory began to replace the farm, the individual artisan's workshop, and the household as the center of production, goods began to become available in profusion.

By historical standards, the goods those factories were manufacturing were aimed at satisfying an entirely new kind of consumer demand. True, the first factories were mills that mass-produced cotton and wool thread, which was then woven into cloth. And clothing, which is the main thing you make out of cloth, certainly qualifies as one of Keynes' "immediate primary needs." But the immediate primary need for clothing can be—and had long been—met by homespun. The demand that mass-produced clothing satisfied was not just for something to wear, but for *more* and *better* things to wear. In short, it was alchemic demand, the demand for goods and services to satisfy needs beyond the basic biological requirements of life—a demand that has since become the very basis of our modern economy.

There are two fundamental types of alchemic demand: *quantity demand* and *quality demand.*

Quantity demand, the more rudimentary of the two, is the consumer's basic desire for more of what he or she already has: more food,

[17]John Kenneth Galbraith, *The Affluent Society,* 4th revised ed. (New York: New American Library, 1985), 107.

[18]Keynes, "Economic Possibilities for Our Grandchildren," 360.

a bigger house, an extra suit of clothing. This kind of demand may seem adolescent and consequently limited but in fact it can reach huge proportions. For example, from 1960 to 1988 the number of homes containing a television set rose from 90 to 98 percent. But the number of homes containing two or more television sets rose from 11 to 60 percent.[19]

If quantity demand can be thought of as the consumer's demand for a larger supply of an existing alchemic product, quality demand reflects the appetite for a different *kind* of product. In the case of television sets, quantity demand manifests itself in terms of a consumer's relatively simple desire to own more than one TV. Quality demand, by contrast, reflects his or her more sophisticated yearning for a *better* TV (say, a big-screen color receiver with remote-control capability and stereo sound) as well as for related but otherwise entirely new products (such as a videocasette recorder, a laser-disc player, and so on).

When Keynes and his successors worried about the likelihood that increasingly prosperous consumers would feel decreasingly motivated to spend, they were thinking mainly in terms of quantity demand. People might well want more food, a bigger house, an extra suit, standard economic logic told them, but there was a limit, wasn't there? After all, no matter how rich you are, you can only drive one car at a time.

Well, yes and no. Wealth may not give you the ability to drive more than one car simultaneously; but if the marketplace provides you with an array of new and better vehicles—say, a Jeep with four-wheel drive, a turbo-charged sports car, and an air-conditioned limousine complete with cellular telephone and CD player—there is no reason for the person of means not to buy all three.

In short, what Keynes and his fellows didn't realize was that when quantity demand is satiated—as it is these days among the vast majority of Americans—quality demand kicks in. When you have all the food, clothing, and TVs you need—as most Americans do today—you start wanting better food, better clothing, and better TVs. To put it another way, the typical middle-class American couple would probably have

[19]1960 television-ownership statistics from *World Almanac and Book of Facts*, 1973 ed. (New York: Pharos Books, 1973), 1032; 1988 statistics from *World Almanac and Book of Facts*, 1989 ed. (New York: Pharos Books, 1989), 356.

little if any interest in buying a third Toyota to add to the two they already own.[20] Far more likely, they would get rid of one of the Toyotas and upgrade to a BMW.

Moreover, this flip in the nature of demand is not one-way. For as the consumer begins to satisfy his or her desire for higher quality, quantity demand once again begins to work its magic. Now the consumer wants *two* BMWs. Theoretically, of course, the demand for more and better goods will be satiated when he or she finally owns a sufficiently large number of the best car available on the market. But as long as technology continues to advance, there never will be a best car—at least not for very long. Each year a better car will be developed, and the process will start all over again.

Less evident but even more pervasive is the way in which quantity and quality demand feed on each other directly. A man gets a better job and buys a better quality suit. Immediately, he needs a better tie, a better shirt, and a better pair of shoes. Then he needs another better quality suit, the acquisition of which causes him to need another new set of accessories—and so on and so on. The reason he needs all these accessories is that, without them, the quality of his new suit will be diminished. In other words, quality is inextricably linked to quantity. This is a fundamental characteristic of alchemic demand; as in the case of one's wardrobe, quantity and quality demand cannot be satisfied separately—either both are met or neither is.

Indeed, many of the new products created by technology are by definition incapable of satiating the demand they create, for they are themselves alchemic demand machines that generate endless loops of continuing consumer need. For example, when a merchant sells a consumer a new Sony Walkman for $50, he is in fact creating far more demand than he is satisfying—in this case a continuing and potentially unlimited need for tape cassettes and batteries. That is, by buying the Walkman, the consumer has not completed a process that began when he first perceived his need for the product; rather, he has merely finished the first cycle of a potentially unlimited series of transactions— in the course of which he may well wind up spending far more each month on the accessories than he did on the original item. The same

[20]By the mid-1980s more than half of all U.S. households could boast at least two cars. From *Statistical Abstract of the United States 1989,* 709.

dynamic applies to a huge range of new products: cars, computers, cameras, VCRs—the list is virtually endless. In purchasing them, consumers in effect are boarding an alchemic train of virtually unlimited demand.

Not every such alchemic demand machine is a new product. Indeed, the most powerful of them all happens to be one of the oldest consumer goods known to humans—the private home. While the purchase of a house or apartment may satisfy the consumer's need for shelter, it also simultaneously generates a wide-ranging series of fresh needs for everything from new furniture to new carpets to new appliances, the acquisition of each in turn creating another round of new demand. This is why the level of housing starts is considered such a key economic indicator: if people are buying houses, it means they will be buying a lot of other things as well.

This fact of alchemic life has enormous implications for every businessperson. Manufacturers and retailers who don't appreciate the extent to which their primary product may actually generate more demand than it satisfies run the risk of defining their businesses much too narrowly, just like the railroad barons of the turn of the century who were left behind because they failed to realize that their business was transportation, not trains and tracks. In recent years, for example, Sony was nearly driven out of the VCR market by rival JVC because of just such a misunderstanding.

When home videocassette recorders were first introduced in the mid-1970s, there were two competing formats, Sony's Betamax system and Matsushita's VHS system. Because of its clear technical superiority, Sony was confident that the Beta format would prevail. JVC, however, recognized that what it was selling wasn't electronic gadgetry but home entertainment—that as big as the direct market for VCRs seemed to be, it was only the tip of a much larger iceberg of potentially unlimited consumer demand for prerecorded tapes. And it was that tape market—which a conventional businessperson might define as a subsidiary market—that would in fact shape the dynamics of the VCR market; consumers were bound to opt for the system that offered them access to the widest range of taped entertainment.

Thus, while Sony tried to prevent competing manufacturers from using its system, JVC went about aggressively licensing hundreds of other firms to produce VHS machines. Before long, the sheer volume of VHS machines flooding the marketplace began to overwhelm the Beta. As a result, software manufacturers began offering a wider selection of tapes in the VHS format than in Beta. That gave consumers an even greater incentive to buy VHS rather than Beta machines—which, in turn, encouraged videotape distributors to tilt their product mix even more heavily in favor of VHS. By 1987, VHS machines were accounting for more than 90 percent of the $5.25 billion U.S. market for VCRs. Sony finally threw in the towel early in 1988, announcing plans to begin manufacturing its own VHS machine.[21]

IBM displayed a similar understanding of alchemic realities in the early 1980s, when it decided to enter the personal-computer market, which up until then was effectively monopolized by Apple. Realizing that consumers bought computers to run software and not the other way around—in other words, that its business wasn't computers but information processing—IBM decided to end its long-held practice of jealously protecting its proprietary technology. Instead, it adopted an "open architecture" for its PC line that positively encouraged competing manufacturers not only to produce software and peripheral equipment for the IBM PC but to build knockoffs of the machine itself. The idea was that the more IBM-compatible machines there were in the marketplace, the more IBM-compatible software would be written—and the more people would buy IBM machines.

Sure enough, despite Apple's superior technology, "IBM-compatible" personal computers became the industry standard—and Big Blue grew more prosperous than ever. Apple, meanwhile, was almost driven out of business. By 1989, it had no choice but to run up the white flag and begin offering an IBM-compatible computer of its own.

Were it not for alchemic demand, our economy would be a tiny fraction of its current size. The fact is, for all that we moan about the high cost of living, if one is simply concerned with mere survival, one *needs* astonishingly little in the way of goods and services. Consider, for example, on how little a homeless street person can manage to subsist: a single set of clothes, a pair of shoes, and a dollar or two a day for food and drink. However you figure it, it's bound to come out to less than $1,000 a year—which is to say, roughly a twentieth of the

[21]Janice Castro, "Goodbye Beta," *Time*, 25 January 1988, 52.

current U.S. per capita gross national product. In other words, some 95 percent of our economy is devoted to filling demand for things that we can literally live without.

This doesn't mean that most of our productive energies today are devoted to essentially superfluous ends. Whether or not they happen to be literally a matter of life and death, our needs are real enough. What takes some getting used to is that fact that, in a society where the majority of the members live significantly beyond the margins of subsistence, perceptions of need are entirely subjective. It is not just in the realm of physics that we have come, in the twentieth century, to find ourselves living in an Einsteinian universe; our economic reality today is no less relativistic than our quantum mechanics or our cosmology. What matters to us in our affluent alchemic world is not the absolute level of our standard of living, but where it stands in relation to other levels: the levels enjoyed by friends and acquaintances, by people (both real and fictional) whom we see on television, by ourselves at some other point in our life. Moreover, there is a kind of ratchet effect to rising standards of living; our current standard, no matter how superior it may be to the standard we enjoyed last year, is invariably and inevitably the minimum we will accept. This is why the fulfillment of what Keynes called our "immediate primary needs" does not shake our thirst for consumption. Rather, it merely becomes the floor for a whole new array of desires.

The alchemic consumer can be thought of as a mountain climber trying to reach the highest peak in an unlimited mountain range in which each mountain he or she climbs turns out to be merely the foothill of another even higher peak. In such a universe, demand can only be satiated when the differential between the level we currently enjoy and all those other levels is one we can regard with satisfaction. Given technology's apparently unlimited ability to keep pumping out new and better goods, there is not much likelihood that more than a tiny fraction of consumers will ever reach that happy state of equilibrium.

This is what Keynes and his many followers failed to see. By asserting that demand was bound to ebb once consumers moved past satisfying their "immediate primary needs" to what he labeled mere "accumulation," Keynes was in effect making a distinction between necessities and luxuries, arguing that people's desire to acquire the former would inevitably be stronger than their desire for the latter. That may sound reasonable enough; after all, it's simply common sense that one's need for food is bound to be more intense than one's need for a Ferrari. But this sort of common sense happens to be wrong. In the alchemic world, the distinction we traditionally make between what we call luxuries and necessities is entirely illusory, for as we have seen, technology is constantly transforming the former into the latter.

My father once told me that when God really wanted to punish someone he would give them everything they asked for—in effect, robbing their life of purpose by removing the need to struggle or achieve. To my father, an immigrant from Eastern Europe who spent his entire life struggling to keep his family financially secure, life was about getting there, not being there.

Perhaps this was what concerned Keynes as he looked to the future from the depths of the Great Depression; perhaps he worried that even worse than the world of want he saw all around him in the 1930s might be the coming world of plenty—a world in which all wants were met and thus a world in which there was nothing more for people to do.

Whatever his motivation, Keynes was wrong in thinking that people would grow sedentary and content in a world with the capacity to fill all of their primary needs—in short, the alchemic world we live in today. His error was in assuming that human satisfaction or happiness was related to some absolute level of achievement. In fact, there is nothing absolute about happiness in our relativistic alchemic world. Rather, it depends on the extent to which reality corresponds to our expectations. To put it in mathematical terms, one could say that *Happiness = Reality − Expectations.* (Or, equally, *Misery = Expectations − Reality.*)

What this means, of course, is that the higher our expectations, the less likely it is that we will be happy (satisfied) and, consequently, the more we will strive to improve our reality. But as we have noted, there is that ratchet effect: the more our reality improves, the higher our expectations go. In alchemic terms, the more demand is satisfied, the larger demand will grow.

The truth of this is evident when we compare how we live today with how we lived, say, twenty years ago. Ever since the energy crisis of the 1970s shook our confidence in the inevitability of material progress, it has been fashionable to assert that the steady upward march of living standards that Americans once took to be their birthright has come to a halt—that our homes used to be bigger, our cars used to be faster, and our hard-earned dollars used to go further.

This couldn't be further from the truth. Over the past twenty or so years, median family income in the United States has more than kept pace with rising prices, which is to say that at the very least, most Americans today can afford to buy more food, shelter, clothing, and other consumer goods than ever before.[22] But that's putting it mildly, indeed. For while most goods are slightly more affordable in relative terms than they used to be, in terms of quality and variety they are vastly superior to what was available twenty years ago.

Consider that classic American luxury-turned-necessity, the television set. In the early 1970s, a top-quality color TV set—say, one with a fifteen-inch screen and automatic color control—cost about $300. In 1989, the same $300 bought you a similar-size color set with a far superior picture tube, infrared remote control, and an electronic tuner capable of bringing in 150 cable, UHF, and VHF channels. Of course, after adjusting for inflation, spending $300 in 1989 was the equivalent of spending just $120 in 1971—meaning that the TV Americans could buy for $300 in 1989 was not only a better-quality set than the $300 1971 model, it was also some 60 percent cheaper in real terms.

This is true of virtually every major consumer item. Whether you are talking about TVs or toys, automobiles or air conditioners, blue jeans or bedding, cameras or convertible sofas, refrigerators or recorded music, Americans today invariably enjoy better quality goods at a lower real cost than they did twenty years ago—or more than any other consumers at any other time in history.[23]

[22]Between 1970 and 1987, the U.S. Bureau of Labor Statistics' overall consumer price index rose 193 percent. (From *Statistical Abstract of the United States 1989*, 469.) In the same period, median family income rose 201 percent. (From U.S. Department of Labor, Bureau of Labor Statistics, *Employment and Earnings.*)

[23]Compare, for example, the $350 seventeen-cubic-foot refrigerator of 1971 with its 1989 counterpart; not only is the modern unit nearly a third cheaper in real terms, it is also 27 percent more energy efficient and offers a variety of "luxury" features (such as an automatic ice-maker) that is predecessor lacked. Or compare a typical 1971-model subcompact car (say, a $2,700 Datsun 510) with its 1989 "equivalent" (say, a $7,500 Ford Escort). Adjusted for inflation, the two cars cost roughly the same. But in terms of amenities, reliability, fuel efficiency, and performance, the 1989 Ford is far superior to the 1972 Datsun.

So why is it that so many people feel they used to have it better? The reason is that as much as the material quality of American life has risen, the expectations of Americans have risen even higher. To use our example of the television set, although today's $300 TV is in every way a better set than 1971's $300 model, it no longer satisfies our demand for quality; advancing technology has raised the level of what we deem acceptable. Thus it is that the consumers who happily purchased $300 TVs twenty years ago are not content to continue buying $300 sets today, even though they are getting higher quality at a significantly lower real cost. Instead of saving money, as Keynes feared they would, most consumers today prefer to spend the same or more in real terms compared to twenty years ago. That is, if they spent the $300 on a TV set in 1971, they spend at least $800 today—in return for which they wind up with a TV that meets the current definition of top quality: a cable-ready, seventeen-inch color set with on-screen digital display, full-function remote control, stereo sound, and built-in programmable timer.

Thus it is, as the statistics show, that our motivation to spend does not slacken once we reach that "margin of comfort" about which Keynes worried. To the contrary, the more we have, the more we need.

The point of all this is simple: whether you are an economist or an entrepreneur, to try to evaluate consumer demand in terms of some fixed definition of people's "real needs" is to look backwards into the past. In the alchemic world of unlimited technology, there is no limit to people's "real needs."

To look at it another way, while economists may argue that what is available is a function of what people want, *the Alchemist recognizes that what people want is a function of what is available.* It's not simply that new products plant new ideas in consumers' minds. Of course, they do that. But they also do something more. They provide consumers with a greater range of choices, and choice happens to be one of the most potent stimulants of demand.

This is evident in the dynamics of that showcase of modern consumer activity, the suburban mall. When self-contained shopping centers first began to sprout in suburban America, many retailers were convinced that setting up shop cheek-by-jowl with competing merchants was bound to be bad for business. In particular, they feared that the concentration of stores would make malls bloody Hobbesian arenas of all-against-all competition in which neighboring retailers would fruit-lessly steal customers from each other to the benefit of no one, not even the shoppers; the shoppers, it was feared, would be exhausted and confused by the vast array of products and services spread out before them.

As it turned out, of course, shopping centers proved to be one of the great marketing and distribution innovations of the past century. Rather than demoralizing shoppers, the profusion of choices offered by the modern mall seemed to energize them. Indeed, to the delight of retailers, experience has shown that as shopping malls increase in size, so does the sales volume per square foot.[24] In short, the more choices consumers seem to have, the faster the total market seems to grow; the more there is available for consumers to buy, the more they *want* to buy.

This phenomenon hasn't just been restricted to shopping centers. When the Coca-Cola Company introduced its New Coke back in 1985, devotees of the original formula responded with a deluge of complaints that ultimately forced the company to bring back the old version under the brand name of Classic Coke. To outsiders (and even to a number of senior Coca-Cola executives), the resulting "two Coke" strategy seemed clear evidence of an embarrassing and potentially ruinous miscalculation. In fact, though, rather than cannibalizing each other's markets, New Coke and Classic Coke together managed to gain a bigger audience than either could have amassed separately. As a result, Coca-Cola's overall share of the $30 billion U.S. soft-drink market climbed from just over 35 percent in 1983 to nearly 41 percent in 1988. When it came to stimulating demand, it appeared, two Cokes were better than one.

Technology's ability to provide us with an ever-widening array of new and better products may seem like an irresistible force. But there is an apparently immovable object with which it must contend: the basic and inherent conservatism of human beings. For all our fascina-

[24]The typical 146,000-square-foot community shopping center averages just over $144 in sales per square foot. By contrast, the typical 360,000-square-foot regional mall averages $179 per square foot. From *Dollars and Cents of Shopping Centers: 1987* (Washington: The Urban Land Institute, 1987), 21, 115.

tion with novelty, we really don't like change; indeed, we resist it even when we know it will be good for us. When it comes down to it, the average person will adopt a new way of doing something only if it is clearly worth the trouble, if the advantages outweigh the disadvantages by a wide margin. To put it in economic terms, he will buy a new product or adopt a new way of doing something only if the cost-benefit ratio is overwhelmingly favorable.

To generations of manufacturers, this fact of human nature meant that in order to succeed in the marketplace a new product not only had to fill a need but it had to do so at a sufficiently attractive price. These twin constraints posed a daunting barrier that made most established companies extremely wary about introducing new products.

This wariness—which once upon a time might have been called prudence—is no longer appropriate. For as we have seen, in our alchemic world new products create their own need. As a result, the only constraint on demand today is price. To put it another way, in an alchemic world of infinitely plastic need, people will buy *anything* if it's cheap enough. Whether it is a Ford Model T or a Toshiba VCR, if the price is right, consumers will suddenly find that they have a need for that crazy newfangled gadget they've been hearing about. In fact, at some price, they'll probably want to acquire more than one. And once they have acquired the gadget, they won't be able to imagine how they ever managed to get along without it.

Of course, the conventional wisdom will tell you that the right price for a consumer may not be the right price for a manufacturer. Sure, you can sell anything if you price it cheaply enough. The question is: can you make a profit in the process?

The economist will answer "not necessarily." The Alchemist, by contrast, knows that because of technology the answer is invariably "yes."

The reason is what is known as the learning curve. As we have seen, because of the alchemic effect of technology, the expense of actual physical materials and manufacturing labor that go into each unit is a relatively small component of the total cost of making most finished products today. Far greater are the fixed expenses—fixed in the sense that they remain the same whether you produce one item or one thousand—of research and development, retooling, marketing, and the like. Because these fixed expenses far exceed the marginal material expense that is attached to each item, the more items you produce, the lower the unit cost of each will be—and the lower the price you can sensibly charge consumers. Of course, the lower the price you can charge, the more demand there will be for your product—and the greater the likelihood that you will be able to sell the huge volume you had to produce in order to achieve the economies you needed.

This may sound circular, but it works. Such is the "magic" of the alchemic power of technology.

The validity of the learning-curve approach was first demonstrated by Robert Noyce and Jeremiah Sanders of Fairchild Semiconductor in the early 1960s, when they employed it to get television manufacturers to start using their new 1211 transistor rather than RCA's "nuvistor" vacuum tube in their UHF tuners.[25] When Fairchild first set out to win the UHF-tuner market, it was making relatively small numbers of the 1211—at a manufacturing cost of about $100 per unit—which it sold mainly to the military at a price of $150 apiece. This $100 cost per unit reflected the sum of two separate costs. First, there was the marginal production cost—that is, the cost of the actual physical materials and manufacturing labor that went into each transistor on the assembly line—of just a few cents per unit. Then there was the fixed overhead cost—that is, the millions of dollars of research and development expense divided by the few thousand or so transistors that they expected to sell—of nearly $100 a unit.

RCA's nuvistor tubes, by contrast, were priced at just $1.05 each.

The dilemma was simple: how could Fairchild convince customers to give up a reliable old technology in favor of a promising but relatively untested new one that at the moment cost about a hundred times more?

The conventional business approach to this problem would have been to give up. No doubt the price of the 1211 would come down as more of the transistors were produced. But could the price be brought down by a factor of a hundred or more? And even if it could, how would you get from here to there? Normally, with new products you started small and hoped they would catch on—that is, you hoped that there

---

[25]The story of Fairchild's successful assault on RCA's nuvistor vacuum tube is dramatically told in George Gilder's excellent book *Microcosm: The Quantum Revolution in Economics and Technology* (New York: Simon and Schuster, 1989), 118–21.

would turn out to be a demand for them. If there was, then volume would increase, unit costs would drop, and eventually you could lower the price, thereby increasing demand further. In this case, however, given the huge price difference between the 1211 and its competition, there was simply no way to start small—no chance that even a single $150 transistor could be sold to the TV industry.

Fairchild, of course, did not take the conventional route and give up. Rather, it decided to short-circuit the process by slashing the price of the 1211 from $150 per transistor to $1.05 apiece at the very beginning—in effect, betting that the enormous cut would spur sufficiently huge demand to justify raising production levels to the point where unit costs would fall low enough to make the effort profitable. "We were going to make the chips in a factory we hadn't yet built, using a process we hadn't yet developed, but bottom line: we were out there the next week quoting $1.05," Sanders later recalled. "We were selling into the future."[26]

The leap of faith more than paid off. Between 1963 and 1965, Fairchild wound up capturing fully 90 percent of the UHF tuner market in the United States. Moreover, by 1965, growing demand for the 1211 had pushed production levels so high—and unit costs so low—that Fairchild was able to cut the price of its transistor to just fifty cents each and still make a hefty profit.

These days this sort of learning-curve pricing is standard practice among smart manufacturers—in particular, the Japanese, who used it to take the VCR market away from the U.S. companies that invented the device. Conventional thinkers resent the technique even as they are steamrolled by it. They call it "dumping" and label those who practice it as unfair traders. In fact, there is nothing at all unfair about learning-curve pricing—except perhaps that in order to see its advantages, you need to recognize a few alchemic facts of life: namely that the level of demand is simply a function of price, and that what determines price is the level of our technology.

This can be stated succinctly as the Fifth Law of Alchemy:

Technology determines the level of consumer demand by determining the price at which goods can be sold.

[26]Gilder, *Microcosm*, 121.

The conventional understanding of the way the marketplace works is that the price a producer can get for an item depends on the level of consumer demand for it. For the conventional businessperson, therefore, the crucial question is: will the price the market is willing to pay for my product exceed the cost of manufacturing it? If it does, the manufacturer will prosper. If it doesn't, he or she will fail. Either way, it's something of a crapshoot.

In our alchemic age of unlimited technology, the reverse is true: the level of consumer demand for a new product depends on the price. For the alchemic businessperson, therefore, the question is whether the technology is good enough to permit setting the price of the product sufficiently low to generate the demand that is needed. Given the accelerating pace of technological advances on the supply side of the alchemic equation, chances are the answer will be yes.

One of the most enduring clichés of entrepreneurial lore is that the way to succeed in business is to figure out what people need and give it to them. As we have seen, this is in fact a recipe for disaster. It's not that a clever businessperson can't find out what sort of products or services are in demand by studying the marketplace. It's that whatever he or she might happen to learn is not likely to be of more than historical interest. After all, just because consumers want something today doesn't necessarily mean they will want it tomorrow. Indeed, if anything, the fact that they want something today practically guarantees that they won't want it tomorrow.

The businessperson who ignores this fact is like a restaurateur who thinks the secret to success is to learn to make one dish so well that his customers will keep coming back for it. The fact is that no matter how brilliantly he prepares that dish—or, for that matter, how attractively he prices it—after two or three nights, his customers are going to want to try something different, even if it is not as good. And if he can't give it to them, they will go somewhere else.

Consumer needs and wants have always been plastic, of course. Still, businesspeople used to be able to get by on riding the coattails of existing demand—that is, by reacting to current market conditions rather than initiating new ones—because until recently the nature and level of consumer demand changed relatively slowly. In recent years, however, the rate of change in the marketplace has begun to accelerate dramatically. And the economic landscape has become littered with the corpses of businesses that couldn't keep up.

Not only are new products coming to market faster than ever before, but existing products are evolving, mutating, and changing at speeds undreamt of just a few years ago. What's behind this frenzy of activity, of course, is the accelerating rate at which technology has been advancing. The key to this acceleration is the explosion in information technology. We have already seen the crucial role the level of information technology plays on the supply side of the alchemic equation. In fact, it plays an even more important role on the demand side.

It goes without saying that a consumer can't conceive a demand for a new product unless and until he or she knows about it. These days, as the technology of mass communications leaps forward—generating everything from on-line computer data services to more sophisticated direct-marketing techniques—word of new products and processes reaches consumers around the world at literally the speed of light. And unlike on the supply side, where the sharing of information is only the beginning of the development process, on the demand side its effect is often instantaneous. There need be no delay between learning of a new product and deciding you need it.

The speed at which technology can—and constantly does—remake the marketplace has fundamentally altered the nature of what constitutes smart business practice. Simply making a good product and cultivating steady customers are not enough anymore. To the contrary, in today's alchemic world, if you have a good product and a clearly identified customer base, you're in trouble. You're in trouble because one of two things is bound to happen: either someone will come up with a way of supplying your product at a lower cost, or some entirely new product will appear that renders yours obsolete.

Indeed, those are the two fundamental routes to business success in the alchemic world: you can either figure out a way to reduce the cost of manufacturing some existing product, or you can come up with an entirely new product.

Traditionally, most businesspeople have focused on the former, and for good reason. For one thing, as business strategies go, it seems a lot less risky to try to improve an existing product than to attempt to develop an entirely new one. After all, existing products imply existing markets; there are already customers out there whose habits and reactions you can study, hard facts—not guesswork—on which you can base your assumptions and fashion your plans. What's more, whether or not it is less risky, it is certainly considerably easier to refine proven old ideas than to come up with good new ones; as difficult and challenging as it may be to figure out more efficient ways of doing things, blazing new trails has always been harder than improving old roads.

The Japanese demonstrated the soundness of this strategy in their early post-World War II development. By lowering the cost of production of a variety of existing products—from cars to computers, steel to supertankers, video recorders to video games—they transformed themselves into an economic powerhouse of gargantuan proportions.

But though there is still plenty of money to be made emulating the early Japanese model, that is a strategy of the past. In our alchemic future, the lion's share of economic growth is bound to come from revolution, not reform. That is, the businesspeople most likely to prosper will be those who devote themselves to developing new products, not those who concentrate on finding ways to lower the production cost of existing ones.

The reason is simple. Given the accelerating pace of change in the marketplace, by the time you have figured out a way to manufacture an existing product more efficiently, chances are that advancing technology will have come up with some entirely new device or process that will make your product totally obsolete, regardless of how much better or more inexpensive you can now make it.

Take, for example, the record business. Despite the continuous and significant improvements in terms of both the price and quality of long-playing vinyl records and stereo turntables—and despite the enormous investment consumers made in records and record-players over the decades—the entire industry is well on its way to extinction. The reason, of course, is the advent of compact-disc technology. By 1989, just five years after they first made their commercial debut, CDs were outselling vinyl records by a hefty margin that was growing wider with every passing day. Similarly, demand for CD-players had almost completely replaced demand for conventional turntables.

The point is that, in the alchemic world, simply making the best product you can is not enough. The excellence of typewriter technology did not cut much ice with consumers when relatively inexpensive word processors began to become widely available. Nor did nearly five hundred years of virtually continuous improvement in the design and manufacture of spring-driven analog watches count for much when quartz-crystal digital technology came along.

In short, what the alchemic businessperson must recognize is that, whether selling cars or clothing or computers or cat food, he or she is fundamentally in the business of change. In a world in which the nature of demand is infinitely plastic (that is, constrained only by the virtually unlimited ability of technology to come up with new products) and the level of demand is potentially unlimited (that is, constrained only by technology's ability to make things cheaply enough), the businessperson must always be on the lookout for what is coming next—and what is coming after that. If Alchemy teaches us anything, it is that there is no end to what people can, will, and must have.

The Japanese seem to have recognized this. Although their original postwar success was built on a traditional economic model—supplying existing products at lower prices—in the 1970s and 1980s they jumped on the alchemic train, shifting their production emphasis from quantity to quality and from emulation to innovation.

In the 1960s, the Japanese overwhelmed many of the world's markets with inexpensive products—in effect, satiating quantity demand. But in the early 1970s they turned their attention to increasing the quality of their goods, riding the alchemic shift from quantity demand to quality demand (leaving the now unprofitable market for cheaper goods to their imitators). In less than twenty years, they went from being known as the lowest-cost producer of almost everything U.S. consumers could want to being known as the highest-quality (and usually the highest-priced) producer of almost everything. In fact by 1990 they were even going after the U.S. consumer who already owned two Toyotas and who could be expected to trade up to a BMW, by introducing two new top-of-the-line automobiles—the Infiniti and the Lexis—whose performance and workmanship exceeded the existing European standards for luxury cars.

We have seen how virtually the whole of our modern economy is built on alchemic demand, the demand for goods and services beyond our physiological requirements. In exploring this demand we have developed the Fourth Law of Alchemy, which explains how technology determines the nature of consumer demand by determining what constitutes a need; and the Fifth Law of Alchemy, which explains how technology determines the aggregate level of demand by determining price (which is determined by the First and Second, or supply-side, Laws of Alchemy). Moreover, we have seen how the speed at which technology advances is determined by the speed with which we process information (the Third Law of Alchemy).

As impressive as all of this analysis may seem, it explains only the past. The question is, can we use our alchemic understanding of the past to determine what the future holds in store for us? The answer is yes. As we shall soon see, by understanding the technology gap, we can use our understanding of what has happened to predict and explain what is about to happen.

THE TECHNOLOGY GAP

In which we define the Sixth Law of Alchemy, which explains how the Theory of Alchemy can help us anticipate the future as well as explain the past.

WHEN EARLY HUMANS first figured out how to control and use fire, they did more than discover a way to keep themselves warm on cold nights. They also laid the basis for a variety of other new technologies—such as cooking, lighting, and the forging of metals—whose development would wind up transforming the nature of human existence. Similarly, when William Shockley, Walter Brattain, and John Bardeen invented the transistor at Bell Laboratories in 1948, they not only gave the world a new and better kind of switching device, they also made possible the whole of modern electronics—telecommunications, computers, sensing devices, automated systems, and all the other new products and processes that are responsible for what we have come to think of as our twentieth-century way of life.

This is a fundamental characteristic of technological progress: new inventions are less ends in themselves than they are links in a continuing chain of innovation. That is, every major breakthrough spurs the development of not just one new device or service but an entire array of fresh products and processes; an advance in one area inevitably provokes advances in other areas. Technology, in short, feeds on itself.

Thus it is that we speak of the multiplier effect of technology. The higher the level of our technology to begin with, the faster that level will rise. As the level rises, the rate of progress escalates—leaping ahead more and more swiftly in an accelerating spiral until it reaches a critical state at which point our technological capabilities can seem to be infinite.

For most of recorded history, the general level of technology was fairly low. Technology thus advanced slowly, puttering along in barely perceptible fits and starts, as did the overall quality of life.

As we noted earlier, it wasn't until the start of the industrial revolution in the early eighteenth century that things began to change noticeably. In part, this was because of the greater productive capacity of the factory as opposed to the farm and the household. Equally if not more important, however, was the widespread implementation of technological advances in communication and transportation. Specifically, the growing sophistication and ubiquity of the printing press and the sailing ship led to a quantum leap in humankind's information-processing ability, which in turn allowed general technology to leap ahead at an unprecedented rate.

Since then technology has been advancing at a faster and faster rate, to the point where, from an economic standpoint, there appears to be very little that it cannot do. Today, even the long-derided goal of the ancient alchemists—to learn how to transmute base metals into gold—is an elementary exercise for nuclear physicists. Indeed, to the non-scientist at least, our technological capabilities seem so limitless that most people tend to assume that all they have to do is ask and technology will deliver. As a result, the process of innovation has been turned on its head. It used to be that an inventor would come up with some new invention and then consumers would figure out whether or not they could use it. Nowadays, we decide in advance what we could use and then we tell the scientists and engineers to invent it.

The first great example of this sort of demand-driven innovation was the Manhattan Project, the United States' four-year, $2 billion effort to develop the atomic bomb during World War II. In giving the go-ahead to the project, President Roosevelt was in effect ordering the nation's scientific establishment to invent a device—namely, a nuclear explosive—that was not only beyond the technological capabilities of the day but that many experts doubted would ever be feasible. The fact was, however, that the nation needed the bomb, and like the prototypical alchemic manager he was, Roosevelt believed in technology's ability to rise to the challenge.

A similar example of expecting technology to adapt to external considerations rather than the other way around was the Apollo Project. When President Kennedy announced in May 1961 that by the end of the decade the United States would land a man on the moon and bring him back safely, the technology necessary to perform such a feat simply did not exist. That, of course, was beside the point. As long as the consumer—in this case, the government—was willing to pay the price, it was assumed that technology could and would deliver. And, in the end, it did.

This is the essence of alchemic management. New Alchemists have such faith in technology that they design products without limiting themselves to the current level of technology. The only consideration they take into account is their reading of the marketplace.

Today, technology is advancing so rapidly that people cannot afford to allow their plans to be limited by what is currently possible. Those who do will not remain in business very long. The key to survival in the fast-changing alchemic world is to keep looking down the road, to anticipate what is likely to come next week, next month, next year—to base your plans on what you think will be, not what already is.

Hindsight, the saying goes, is always 20/20. The problem is that what seems obvious in retrospect—that Polaroid was a great investment in 1938, that OPEC couldn't hold together, that the Jets would beat the Colts in Super Bowl III—is rarely so clear in advance. The question is, how do you know what to anticipate? How does the Alchemist figure out which of the myriad possibilities he or she faces at every juncture is most likely to pan out?

The answer lies in understanding what we call the technology gap.

The term *technology gap* has traditionally been used to describe the disparity in technological sophistication between the United States and Western Europe, or between the industrialized West and the Third World. As we shall see, however, the significance of this sort of gap—though it continues to obsess some politicians and policymakers—is relatively trivial. What really matters is not the technology gap that exists *between* societies but the one that exists *within* each society; not the gap between us and them, but the gap between what is and what could be. This is the technology gap on which Alchemists focus—the gap, as a 1976 Brookings Institution report defined it, "between the best production practice possible with current knowledge and the practice in actual use."[1]

The profound significance of this gap is obvious when we consider the nature of progress. What accounts for progress? That is, how has humanity managed to improve its way of life over the millennia? At its most basic level, the answer involves technology. Very simply, the world had progressed by finding and implementing better ways of doing things.[2] Using flints to make sparks was a better way of getting a fire going than waiting for a random lightning strike to set a tree ablaze. Using sticks to kill animals was a better hunting technique than trying to bring them down by hand. Domesticating livestock and planting crops was a better way of getting food than merely hunting and gathering.

It is no accident that we literally define historical eras by their technology—the Stone Age, the Bronze Age, the Iron Age, the Industrial Age, and so forth. After all, technology is what distinguishes one era from another, one way of life from another. Traditional economics may view technological advance as a by-product of economic growth, but the fact is—as the Alchemist recognizes—that economic growth is a by-product of technological advance.

Why was it that, as Keynes observed, the standard of living enjoyed by most of the world's population hardly changed at all from roughly 2000 B.C. to the beginning of the eighteenth century? One obvious answer is that this was a period in which technology advanced slowly if at all.

Of course, there were during this 3,700-year epoch a few relatively brief and localized spurts of rapid economic growth, during which living standards rose (at least for a while). Invariably, however, these surges followed periods that saw significant technological break-

[1]The Brookings Institution, *Asia's New Giant: 1976* (Washington: The Brookings Institution, 1976), 527. Despite its excellent definition of the technology gap, this report—like virtually every other on the subject—focused mainly on the differences between U.S. and Japanese technology.

[2]In this context, *better* means more efficient (that is, cheaper), more effective, or both.

throughs. Ancient Egypt, for example, achieved great heights of wealth and power as a result of its development of new agricultural techniques (specifically, irrigation and warehousing). Similarly, the great empires of Renaissance Europe came to dominate the world as a result of innovations in navigation and munitions. And when technology finally broke loose in the industrial revolution, the result was a long-term global expansion that transformed the world from one in which only kings enjoyed luxuries to one in which every person could live in a fashion better than former kings.

The fact is, technology has always been the major determinant of humankind's level of progress. The reason this has not been fully appreciated is that technology usually advanced so slowly that its effect was rarely obvious over the course of a single lifetime. Even when major technological breakthroughs were made—say, the invention of the wheel or the development of irrigation—news of the development generally spread so slowly and gradually that most people perceived of the new product or process as something someone else already had rather than as something new that was just invented. Moreover, few if any of these breakthroughs were the work of a single person or even a single generation. They usually evolved over time with each user adding his or her own modification to the concept. It is not surprising then that until this century, technology was considered an invisible constant in economic growth. Whereas the alchemic equation for wealth $(W = PT^n)$ recognizes the overwhelming importance of technology, it has traditionally been thought that wealth was simply a function of physical resources, rather than one of physical resources *and* technology. Thus it is that, in their desire for wealth, people and societies have usually strived, not for more technology, but for more physical resources—which they would usually try to wrest from some other individual or nation by means of force.

Ironically, the one time in which technology has tended to advance rapidly enough for its significance to be apparent has been wartime. Overall, there is no field of human activity in which the significance and power of technology is more self-evident than the military arena. Ever since David employed a slingshot to bring down Goliath, right through Archimedes' development of the catapult in the Second Punic War (which helped keep the besieging Roman legions from overrunning the city of Syracuse in 212 B.C.), to the dropping of the atomic bomb in 1945, the major determinant of military victory has almost always been technology. Though intangibles like morale and courage are obviously important, the winning side in a battle or war is invariably the one with the better technology.[3] Certainly, endless books on military history conclude that the story of warfare is, more than anything else, the story of advancing technology.

Interestingly enough, the most significant advances in military technology have generally not involved weapons *per se,* but rather reflected developments in a given society's prevailing technological infrastructure—in particular, its ability to communicate. Military historian Martin Van Creveld has pointed out, for example, that the "large, permanent, centrally directed armies . . . of the Egyptian, Sumerian, Assyrian, Chinese, Indian, Hellenistic, and Roman Empires would have been inconceivable [had it not been for the invention of] writing." Similarly, as Van Creveld has noted, the main determinant of "the maximum size [of] individual tactical units" is the nature of an army's means of communications—whether its soldiers stay in touch with one another via bugles, flags, or radios.[4]

This is yet another example of the critical importance of information technology. As always, it is the level of information technology that more than anything else sets the rate at which overall technology advances.

In any case, it is only in recent times—that is, over the last few decades—that technology has begun advancing with sufficient speed and breadth for its significance as the major determinant of growth to become apparent. Lately, of course, it has been advancing so quickly that we can barely keep up with it. Indeed, when we consider the matter, it doesn't take long to realize that we are *not* keeping up—that technology is progressing so rapidly that we are simply unable to make use of everything it offers us.

How many of us, after all, drive a car outfitted with the latest computerized fuel injection system, or live in a house built with the

---

[3]One might argue that both the U.S. experience in Vietnam and the Soviet experience in Afghanistan disprove this. In fact, while U.S. and Soviet weaponry may have been more powerful in a conventional sense than that of the Viet Cong and the Afghan rebels, it was not technologically superior; at the very least, in both cases the superpowers' technology was inappropriate to the terrain and circumstances.

[4]Martin Van Creveld, *Technology and War* (New York: The Free Press, 1989), 37–40.

latest ceramic fiber insulation, or watch Johnny Carson on a television set with the latest high-definition digital picture tube? How many manufacturers use nothing but the latest state-of-the-art CAD/CAM techniques to fabricate their products? How many distributors have fully outfitted all their warehouses with the latest automated materials-handling equipment? How many retailers track their inventory and monitor customer preferences with the latest point-of-sale laser scanning devices?

The answer, of course, is not many.

This is the essence of the technology gap. Since the beginning of recorded history, there has never been a society that was as efficient, effective, or productive as it was capable of being—capable not in some theoretical or idealistic sense, but capable in terms of the technology it possessed but for one reason or another did not use. In short, no society has ever—in economic terms, at least—lived completely up to its potential. The degree to which a given society falls short of that potential at any given time—that is, the degree to which the advance of technology outstrips a particular society's ability or willingness to make use of the latest developments and breakthroughs—is the measure of its technology gap.

At first glance, it might seem that the societies with the narrowest technology gaps would be in some sense the most desirable societies. After all, didn't our parents teach us that one should always live up to one's potential? The fact is, however, that societies with relatively narrow technology gaps contain far less potential for growth than societies with wide technology gaps.

As it happens, no society in history has ever had a technology gap as wide as that of modern America and its industrialized peers in Europe and Asia. The reason our technology gap is so wide is not that we are reluctant to adopt the latest technological advances (though, in fact, we are not always as eager to do so as we could be). Rather, it is because technology is simply advancing too quickly for us to keep up with it.

Technology gaps exist on many levels: in precisely the same way that we can discuss the technology gap of an entire society, so too can we talk about the technology gap in the life-style of a specific individual or in the operations of a given company or institution. Whether we are dealing with people, companies, or societies, all have particular tasks

us a new and better way of accomplishing some particular job. In a slower-paced, more settled world, a businessman might be able to afford to wait for the salesman to come to him with news of his latest products. Not so in our alchemic world of accelerating change. If our widget-manufacturer had been an Alchemist, he would have been on the phone every other week (if not more often), not just with his computer salesman but with the salesman's competitors, trying to find out what new developments in widget-making technology were coming down the pike. In short, Alchemists don't wait for the better way to find them; they are constantly out there actively looking for it.

We have seen in the First and Second Laws of Alchemy how technology determines the definition and supply of physical resources, in the Fourth and Fifth Laws of Alchemy how technology determines the nature and level of consumer demand, and in the Third Law of Alchemy how information technology controls the advance of the overall level of technology. Thus having explained how technology is the major determinant of economic activity, we have arrived at our final and Sixth Law of Alchemy:

The immediate economic potential for an individual, an industry, or a society can be explained by examining the technology gap, the best practices possible with current knowledge, and the practices in actual use.

We can call the better way for which the Alchemist is always searching a Ready-to-be-Implemented Technological advance, or an R-I-T. An R-I-T isn't a pipe dream or an item on a wish list. It is a new product or process that is available to us today. It's just that, out of ignorance or indolence, we haven't yet got around to making use of it. A list of current R-I-Ts would include the computerized fuel injectors that haven't yet replaced mechanical carburetors, the radial tires that haven't yet replaced standard bias-ply models, the electronic calculators that haven't yet replaced mechanical ones, the electric typewriters that haven't yet replaced manual ones, and the push-button phones that haven't yet replaced rotary models. It might also include the word processors that haven't yet replaced electric typewriters—though not necessarily all of them, since word processors are not yet cost-effective for all users, especially when one considers the cost of training or replacing personnel who cannot or will not learn to use them.

Newness alone does not necessarily indicate the existence of an R-I-T. Before we jump to any conclusions about a particular new product or process, we must first examine all of its interrelated attributes, such as its efficiency, cost, and reliability. A product has to be more than just new; it has to be both new *and* better—and it's not likely to be better unless it happens to be cost-effective. Moreover, even if it is cheaper and easier to use, it might not be reliable enough. And the sum total of all of its various advantages and disadvantages might not be the same for each user.

Above all, what makes an R-I-T literally "ready to be implemented" is that it is *user transparent*—that is, from the standpoint of the skills required for its use, it is virtually the same as the product it is meant to replace. As far as the user is concerned, the only thing that has changed is that a job that used to be more difficult now seems easier. For example, from the driver's point of view, there's no difference between getting behind the wheel of a car with a computerized fuel injection system and one with a mechanical carburetor—except that the fuel-injected car has a lot more power and gets twice the gas mileage. Similarly, if you know how to use a rotary phone, you can use a push-button model without learning any new skills—yet you will be able to dial faster and more accurately. So too with an electric versus a manual typewriter.

Of course, not all technological advances are user transparent when they are first introduced. In fact, most aren't. Take, for example, the electronic calculator. Unquestionably, the modern electronic calculator is better at manipulating figures than the mechanical adding machine. It's more reliable, easier to use, and considerably less expensive. To the extent, therefore, that there are still people using mechanical calculators who could just as easily and cheaply (indeed, *more* easily and cheaply) be using electronic calculators, the device represents an R-I-T. To put it another way, there is today a real technology gap when it comes to calculators—the gap being a function of the number of mechanical calculators still in use today that could sensibly be replaced by electronic ones.

The clear superiority of the electronic calculator over its mechanical predecessor may seem obvious today. But that was not apparent until relatively recently. When they were initially introduced in the 1960s, the first generation of desktop electronic calculators were far more expensive than the mechanical adding machines they were meant to replace. What's more, not only did those early models require specialized training, but they lacked the old mechanical machines' capacity to print out their calculations on rolls of paper. As a result, they represented an R-I-T only to the relatively small number of people whose calculation requirements justified the extra cost, who could efficiently learn to use them, and who didn't need a printed audit trail of their work. In fact, although the electronic calculator was in wide use by the end of the 1970s, it wasn't until the 1980s—with the development of efficient roll-paper printers and operating systems that mimicked the mechanical products they replaced—that the electronic calculator became sufficiently transparent that it could be reasonable regarded as an R-I-T for virtually every potential user.

Some new products never become user transparent; that is, however much their design is refined, they continue to require new and different operating skills than the devices they are meant to replace. They can still achieve the status of an R-I-T, however, if their cost-effectiveness is great enough to justify the time and trouble it takes to learn new operating skills. This was the case with the word processor, which, as it happens, seems to be becoming user transparent to a whole new generation of typists who have never even used an electric typewriter.

Overall, we can look at a specific office as a factory for processing information and say that its technology gap is the sum of the R-I-Ts it could sensibly employ but for one reason or another hasn't gotten around to installing—that is, the word processors, push-button telephones, and electronic calculators it hasn't yet bought to replace its typewriters, rotary phones, and mechanical adding machines. Similarly, we can look at a specific oil-drilling operation and say that its technology gap is the sum of the better but so far unimplemented drill-rig components, power supplies, and transportation systems that it could utilize on a cost-effective basis. (It should be noted, by the way, that R-I-Ts don't necessarily manifest themselves in the form of equipment of one sort or another. An R-I-T could just as easily reflect itself in terms of a better organizational structure, a better training procedure, or even just one better manager.)

Though they probably wouldn't put it in these terms, today's smart entrepreneurs almost universally look for the existence of R-I-Ts when deciding what new businesses to enter. That is, they recognize instinctively that in the modern Alchemic world there is no point in trying to get into some particular business unless they have some "better way" of doing it—in other words, unless there is an R-I-T that they can implement or develop.

The logic is quite simple. The more R-I-Ts in a particular business, the wider its technology gap; the wider its technology gap, the greater its potential for growth.

How does the Alchemist tell whether or not there are R-I-Ts out there waiting to be exploited? He or she analyzes the business in precisely the same way as we earlier analyzed the technology gap of my life-style. That is, he or she studies each and every component of the business, from the efficiency of its equipment to the way it trains its people to its system of handling correspondence, to see whether or not each particular operation utilizes the most advanced technology available. In other words, he or she looks for the existence of individual technology gaps. The sum of these individual gaps is the business's overall technology gap.

Though we may take it for granted as basic common sense, this approach represents a profound departure from traditional business practice. Before the turn of the twentieth century, when technology advanced far more slowly than it does now, you could make it in business simply by being competitive. All you had to do was be as good as your rivals and you would attract your share of the market. Growth was mainly driven by population increase and classic economic demand for existing goods and services.

These days, by contrast, it is the prospect of providing new and better products and services—that is, the implementation of R-I-Ts—that drives most startups. After seven or eight decades of rapid and continuously accelerating change, consumers have no patience anymore with the status quo. Therefore, when it comes to starting a new business today, it is simply not enough to say that you are going to be just as good as the competition. You have got to be able to promise that you are going to provide your particular product or service better, cheaper, or faster—and preferably all three.

An understanding of the technology gap can tell us more than where the best business opportunities happen to be; it may not be an overstatement to say that most of history can be explained by examining the nature of the technology gap—that is, the amount and type of

R-I-Ts—at a given time and place. The fact is, whether one is looking at ancient Rome or modern Europe, what played a major role at every significant juncture was invariably a consequence of the technology gap: the emergence of a better way of doing something (whether making fabric or making war) that quickly superseded existing methods and, in so doing, altered a whole network of social, political, and economic relationships.

Consider, for example, the American Revolution. Why was it that the humanistic ideals of the Age of Enlightenment found their most brilliant and enduring expression in the American colonies of the late eighteenth century? It wasn't as if the modern concepts of liberty, equality, and brotherhood were unknown in Europe at the time. Indeed, Europe was where they were invented—by the likes of Locke, Mill, and Rousseau. Yet the English revolt took a very different form, and the French Revolution ultimately failed. What was it that made America different? What accounts for the fact that modern liberal democracy found a far more hospitable home in the rough, unfettered New World than in the comfortable and sophisticated precincts of the Old?

One could argue that what gave colonial America a leg up on modernity was the vastness of its technology gap relative to that of Europe. Because it was recently settled, because it lacked an established infrastructure, because it possessed an abundance of resources and a paucity of means to process them, America's appetite for innovation, for new and better ways of doing every sort of thing, was huge. Thus, while jaded Europe toyed provocatively with democracy, exuberant America eagerly embraced it as an R-I-T.

The same situation existed in reverse after World War II. After six years of war on a scale never before seen in world history, Europe was devastated, its infrastructure in ruins, its capital stock depleted. Its technology gap, on the other hand, was enormous—which is why today, nearly half a century later, Europe seems poised to pass the United States as an economic powerhouse.

This is not to suggest that backwardness or devastation is necessarily a good thing. (If it were, the less developed countries would by definition be better off than the developed ones.) True, as we noted earlier, the wider a society's overall technology gap, the more opportunity for growth there is in that society. This is why we think of a wide technology gap as a positive indicator, as a kind of capital asset that when and if exploited will result in economic growth. But there are gaps and there are gaps. It is one thing when the gap exists—as it does these days in the industrialized West or as it did in eighteenth-century America—because technology is advancing more rapidly than a particular society can implement it. That is a sign of a socioeconomic health and vitality. But the existence of a technology gap can also be a sign of a moribund society—one in which technology is standing still while the ability to make use of it is actually declining.

Take the case of Brazil. In the early and mid-1970s, the conventional wisdom had it that the sun was setting on the major powers of the industrialized West. The United States, Japan, and Western Europe might have huge economies, the thinking went, but they were mature and played out. The future, it was said, belonged to less developed but faster-growing countries like Brazil.

Indeed, Brazil was supposed to become the economic powerhouse of the 1980s and 1990s, the U.S.A. of the twenty-first century. The reason was its amazing resources: its vast mineral reserves, its fertile soil, and its huge labor force.

Needless to say, that has not happened yet. For all its assets, Brazil today remains a nation caught in poverty and broken dreams, its foreign debt the largest in the world. The conventional explanation for Brazil's failure to live up to everyone's expectations is that it lacked the infrastructure—the roads, the financing institutions, the skilled workers—to properly exploit its resources. This is true as far as it goes, but Brazil's problem went deeper than that. What Brazil really lacked was a *positive* technology gap. It had a technology gap all right, but not one caused by a tidal wave of upcoming innovation. Rather, Brazil's technology gap was the result of a combination of slow (often nonexistent) technological advance and a declining ability to make use of existing technology. To put it another way, because of the lack of an infrastructure, not only were Brazil's resources meaningless, but it possessed an insufficient amount of R-I-Ts.

This is true of much if not all of the Third World. Virtually all of the most advanced accoutrements of modern life that we think of as R-I-Ts—from computers to state-of-the-art sanitation systems—are, in fact, *not* ready to be implemented by the less developed nations. For one thing, in societies that by Western standards are technologically illiterate, they are not user transparent. For another, given the need for massive education, they are not particularly cost-effective.

The economies that wound up prospering in the 1980s, of course, were precisely the ones that the "experts" had expected to decline—those of the United States, Japan, and Western Europe. As it happened, the very thing that had mistakenly been thought to be the fatal weakness of these economies—that is, their "maturity"—turned out to be their strength. Their well-developed infrastructures, their educated and sophisticated consumer populations, and their almost jaded familiarity with change constitute just the conditions it takes to develop a huge supply of R-I-Ts. An Alchemist would have seen it from the beginning: given that it possessed the widest and best possible type of technology gap, the industrialized West was bound to continue expanding throughout the 1980s and beyond.

The kind of negative technology gap that hinders the Third World today bedeviled Europe in the century and a half following the great plague of 1347. That, too, was a time when the technology gap widened because of declines in the utilization of existing know-how rather than in the expansion of what was possible. In fact, right up until the eighteenth century, the overall global technology gap—which widened and narrowed over time in parallel with the rise and fall of the great civilizations—was the result of almost as many declines in technology usage as of new discoveries. That changed (at least in Western Europe and North America) with the advent of the industrial revolution, after which the gap was virtually always caused by the increase in the amount of new technological discoveries rather than declines in society's ability to implement them. (Not incidentally, it was this steady rise in worldwide implemented technological advances, almost totally independent of the continuing rise and fall of the great powers, that was responsible for the profound improvement in the average Westerner's standard of living over the last three centuries.)

What caused this change in the nature of the technology gap? In a phrase, it was the revolution in the technology of information processing—that is, the technology of recording information combined with the technology of transporting it—that sprang directly from the dramatic advances in printing and shipping that had become ubiquitous by the beginning of the eighteenth century.

Gutenberg's printing press may have been developed in the fifteenth century, but it was not until the early 1700s that printed matter became widespread enough to affect the everyday life of the ordinary man. Similarly, though ocean-going vessels had existed from ancient times, and had been refined throughout the sixteenth and seventeenth centuries, it was not until the eighteenth century that worldwide shipping of virtually everything began to have an impact on ordinary life. Perhaps most significant, the combination of these two areas—ubiquitous communication and widespread transportation—took the power to control technological advances away from the tightly knit oligarchies that dominated society and put it into the hands of individuals, whoever and wherever they might be.

There is, of course, a difference between the way we experience technology gaps today and the way our ancestors did centuries ago. The difference is a matter of self-consciousness. Back in what we now call the Stone Age or the Iron Age, people didn't think of themselves as living in a Stone or Iron age. Indeed, they didn't think of themselves as living in any particular age at all. Making that sort of distinction would have seemed pointless to them, as it would have to most of humankind for most of its history, because until relatively recently the vast majority of people thought of themselves as living pretty much the way people had always lived and always would live. The idea of change just wasn't in most people's vocabularies. Still less was the concept of progress. The notion that a different—not to mention a better—age was coming was simply inconceivable to the mass of humankind.

Today, of course, what's inconceivable is the notion of a static world. Unlike our ancestors, we expect things to change. Indeed, notions of change and progress are an integral part of modern people's worldview. Moreover, we recognize the agent of that change: technology. That's hardly surprising, for we have watched technology remake the world before our very eyes.

As a result, we are self-conscious about change in ways that our ancestors never were. We may not be able to anticipate what particular shape it will take, but we know that change of some sort is coming. It always has and it always will. Indeed, we pride ourselves on our ability to cope with change—to go with the flow, so to speak, to roll with the punches.

The new Alchemists, of course, don't just roll with the punches. As we have seen, they stay on top of change, managing it, orchestrating it, manipulating it to their advantage. In the context of business, they do this by studying their industry (or the industry they are thinking of entering) to see if there exists a technology gap to exploit. In other words, they look to see if the current practice in their industry represents the best available way of doing things. If it doesn't, that means there must be some R-I-T out there that they can adopt. This is precisely what virtually all successful modern businesspeople do. (Actually, they have no choice; the capital markets are no longer willing to finance companies that don't.)

The only problem with this approach to business is that, as we saw in the parable about the widget-maker, technology does not stand still. No sooner have you identified a better way of doing something, drawn up your plans, trained your people in the new method and implemented it than an entirely new and better way invariably comes along. It is a lesson that every successful modern businessperson has learned. As Leslie Wexner, chairman of The Limited, a hugely successful specialty chain, noted in bold type in his company's 1989 annual report: "The key is OUR ABILITY TO CHANGE."[5]

When an Alchemist finds and implements a better way of doing something, he or she keeps in mind the fact of its impending obsolescence. This is just what computer hardware and software manufacturers do. Hardware makers put extra expansion slots into their machines for circuit boards that haven't yet been designed or even envisioned, while software designers routinely build upgrade capabilities into their programs. But the computer business is hardly typical; few businesspeople think more than one product generation ahead.

As we have seen, one can develop a reliable model of tomorrow's opportunities by studying today's R-I-Ts. But modeling tomorrow isn't enough. What about the day after tomorrow? How can the Alchemist get a fix on that?

The answer lies in what we might call our Basic Research Technological advances, or B-R-Ts. Just as studying and understanding the nature of our R-I-Ts can provide us with a reliable picture of what's around

[5]Bill Saporito, "Retailing's Winners & Losers," *Fortune,* 18 December 1989, 69–78.

the corner, analyzing our B-R-Ts gives us a preview of what we can expect over the next hill.

What are B-R-Ts? As we noted at the beginning of this chapter, real advances in technology are not so much ends in themselves as they are links in a continuing chain of innovation. To put it another way, it's not simply that today's breakthrough will be superseded by tomorrow's; it's that today's breakthrough will become the building block for tomorrow's. This is the multiplier effect of technology: every new development that we can identify as an R-I-T quickly (if not immediately) becomes the basis for a whole array of brand new technologies. It becomes, in other words, a B-R-T. Over time that B-R-T yields a new R-I-T, which in turn generates a new B-R-T, which eventually produces another R-I-T, and on and on, the process accelerating and widening with each cycle until it seems to be continuous.

As an example, let's examine the development of a particular technological advance. Say, as actually happened, that a development laboratory discovers that silicon is a better semiconductor than germanium. This discovery becomes the basis of a B-R-T, which the development laboratory spends the next several years refining. Eventually, the laboratory figures out a way of designing and manufacturing a new silicon semiconductor. As the laboratory's finished product, this new knowledge constitutes a new R-I-T.

Once the existence of this new R-I-T becomes known, five other companies, each of which happens to manufacture germanium transistors, quickly glom onto it, using it as the B-R-T to develop a new finished product of their own, namely silicon transistors. The development lab's R-I-T, in other words, becomes the B-R-T of the transistor makers, who use it to create a second new R-I-T.

Now each of the five transistor makers has, say, twenty customers who use transistors in the manufacture of circuit boards, oscillators for TV sets, thermostats, fuel-injector controllers, and other components. To these one hundred component makers, the new silicon transistors represent a new B-R-T, which they can use to develop new and better circuit boards, TV oscillators, thermostats, fuel-injector controllers, and so forth.

And the process continues. The improved components represent yet another new R-I-T, which in turn can be exploited as a B-R-T by thousands of consumer-goods manufacturers to produce a new generation of better computers, televisions, automobiles, and other products.

On and on it goes, one sector's new R-I-Ts becoming the basis of another sector's new B-R-Ts, those new B-R-Ts in turn leading to the development of still other new R-I-Ts, technology feeding on itself in an endless upward spiral. Where it will all end—if, indeed, it ever *will* end—is impossible to say. But by keeping an eye on the current round of B-R-Ts, the Alchemist can stay at least two steps ahead of the current game. And in our fast-changing alchemic world staying two steps ahead may well be the bare minimum necessary for survival.

We can thus see our economic future, a future of unlimited wealth coming from our enormous technology gap. And yet our technology gap is not everyone's technology gap. For today most of our R-I-Ts require a higher and higher level of technological infrastructure, more and more previously implemented R-I-Ts, to be an R-I-T. The fuel injector that doubles our supply of energy isn't an R-I-T to a nation without roads or automobiles. The machine that converts ten workers into one machine supervisor, and then improves productivity so much that the nine other workers can also have better jobs, isn't an R-I-T to the worker not educated enough to become a supervisor of machines.

In the past, when the world's technological infrastructure was fairly uniform, most new inventions were implicitly designed to be implemented by societies everywhere. But today our world is bifurcating as we seem to be developing better ways of doing things that are only useful by either a developed technological society or an educated worker, or both.

The poor in the United States are getting poorer and poorer and working less and less, while the majority of the citizens are getting richer and richer and working more and more. The conventional economic wisdom of elasticity in the labor supply no longer seems to apply as each year we have more and more unfilled jobs requiring skilled workers, and more and more unskilled workers requiring jobs. Conventional economics holds that *eventually* more workers would obtain the skills required to get the unfilled jobs, and *eventually* the number of unskilled jobs would rise as the price fell for unskilled labor. But this *eventuality* seems to be moving further and further away.

Moreover, outside the United States, the Third World nations of the world are falling off the edge. As recent as the 1970s we were convinced that these nations, with abundant physical resources like oil, bauxite, and tin, would be able to use their natural resources to become economically prosperous. Instead, following obsolete economic theories based on scarcity they attempted to artificially control the prices for their resources through cartels—accelerating the alchemic process that would have happened anyway—which caused their customers to either develop substitutes for their resources or reduce their dependency on them, or both. As already mentioned, between just 1980 and 1985 the prices in the International Monetary Fund's thirty-product index—in effect, the capital of the Third World—fell 74 percent, many falling to their lowest level in half a century. The previous economic doctrine of scarcity in commodity prices, a doctrine that these countries relied heavily upon in planning their future, no longer holds true for an alchemic world in which no single product is scarce. Thus, on an international as well as an individual scale, the rich are getting richer and the poor are getting poorer.

But all is not lost for both the poor of our society and the Third World. As we shall see in the remaining chapters, many, if not most, of their economic problems come from well-meaning leaders applying obsolete economic theories to their countries' crises. And once we understand the Theory of Alchemy, we can modify our existing policies and develop new ones to bring everyone into the alchemic world. A world of unlimited economic opportunity and prosperity for all.

LABOR IS CAPITAL

WHEN THOMAS JEFFERSON wrote those words he certainly wasn't talking about potential employees. In fact, from the standpoint of potential employers, who voluntarily pay wages of $8,000 per year to one individual and $800,000 to another, the only thing self-evident is that nothing could be farther from the truth.

Ever since the dawn of the industrial revolution, in terms of production, people have been and are becoming more and more unequal. Yet in evaluating the contribution of labor to production, classic economics generally assumed that each laborer is equal in his or her work output over a fixed period of time.

In 1936, John Maynard Keynes recognized that this was not the case. In defining the unit of labor in his book, *The General Theory of Employment, Interest, and Money,* Keynes abandoned the then-classic labor unit of man-hour or man-day, noting "the obvious fact of great differences in the specialized skill of individual workers."[1] In its place, Keynes substituted the wage dollar, under the assumption that "[in a

[1]John Maynard Keynes, *The General Theory of Employment, Interest, and Money* (New York: Harcourt Brace Jovanovich, 1964), 41.

free market] the remuneration of the workers is proportional to their efficiency."[2] For Keynes, the man earning $10 an hour performing a service produced twice as much output as the man earning $5 an hour doing the same service. This seems obvious to us today, but it was a major breakthrough in recognizing that labor is not a homogeneous commodity.

What Keynes was not overly concerned with at the time are perhaps the most important questions concerning us today, namely why one worker is able to produce twice the output of another, and what each of us can do to become that worker. The answer to these questions for labor can be found in examining the same powerful, ubiquitous, and underestimated force that explained our supply of physical resources: technology.

In classic economics, the production of goods and services is determined by the "production function"—the number of units of labor and capital (already-produced goods that are used in the production of other goods) that are required to produce a product or service. The economic objective is to maximize production (or minimize cost) by choosing the optimal combination of labor and capital, assuming that technological change is a "constant."[3] But the Theory of Alchemy teaches us that we cannot hold technology constant in our decision-making process. Technology is a third dimension of the production function and is the variable with the greatest impact, for it determines the basic value of the capital. And, equally important as we shall see, technology also determines the basic value of the labor.

In Chapter 2 we explained how technology determines our definition and supply of physical resources, and how information-processing technology determines our advance of technology. In mathematical terms we expressed this as $W = PT^n$, where W equals wealth, P equals physical resources, and T equals technology. A modified version of this relationship holds true for labor, where W equals the value of our individual or societal labor, P equals the productive value of a person(s)

---

[2] Keynes, *The General Theory of Employment, Interest, and Money,* 42.

[3] The world's most popular textbook on economics defines the production function as "the technical relationship between the maximum amount of output that can be produced by each and every set of specified inputs (or factors of production). It is defined for a given state of technical knowledge." Paul Samuelson and William D. Nordhaus, *Economics,* 12th ed. (New York: McGraw-Hill, 1985), 580.

at a given point in time, and T equals the level of technological advance, which for people equals the level of their education. And just as technological advances in information processing multiply on each other, advances in education for individuals have a similar exponential effect and are the key to increasing the value of labor.

This is the essence of alchemic labor theory. Just as capital, be it physical resources or machines, is defined and controlled by technology, so is labor. And not only does labor respond to investment as does capital, in the alchemic world *capital is increasingly substitutable for labor.* To paraphrase John Kenneth Galbraith, who said that in the affluent society no useful distinction can be made between luxuries and necessities, in the alchemic society no useful distinction can be made between labor and capital. In fact, as we shall see, in the alchemic world, for decision-making purposes, labor *is* capital.

In classic economics, and until just the last few decades, all products and services were created by combining both labor and capital. However, as technology has advanced, increased automation has caused the labor component of finished products and services to decline steadily.

For example, a $100 manufacturing cost of a mechanical watch in 1920 might have consisted of $50 in variable labor cost (that is, a watchmaker was paid $50 for each watch produced) and $50 in capital costs ($25 in fixed capital costs: the overhead on the factory allocated to each watch which had to be paid whether or not any watches were produced; and $25 in variable capital costs: the case, gears, and other components that were purchased from other companies only for each watch produced).

During the next fifty years, in order to lower costs to remain competitive, the manufacturer streamlined and redesigned the manufacturing process to automate or eliminate as many functions as possible. As a result, the $10 manufacturing cost of a mechanical watch in 1970 might have consisted of only $2 in variable labor costs and $8 in capital costs.

By 1980, the manufacturer had converted to digital quartz watches, building a fully automated assembly line where virtually no human being touched the watch during the manufacturing process. As a result, the $1.25 manufacturing cost of the watch included effectively *nothing* in variable labor cost and fully $1.25 in capital costs ($1 in fixed capital costs: the $1 million in up-front factory and design costs allocated to the 1 million watches produced each year; and 25¢ cents in variable capital costs: the case, semiconductor chip, and battery that were purchased from other companies only for each watch produced).

Today, there are many products produced with similar automated manufacturing methods that have virtually no variable labor cost. As the price of skilled labor has increased, and the price of computerized machines has decreased, companies have turned more and more to replacing individual jobs with machines and have designed wholly new production methods that use more machines and fewer people per product produced.

To many people, automation—the replacement of workers with machines—is scary. These people, often called Luddites in reference to early nineteenth-century English workers who destroyed textile machinery,[4] are concerned about the impact on society of people being put out of work by the advance of technology. But their fears are unfounded, because every time a worker is replaced by a machine, society as a whole is no less poor, and is usually richer.

Let's consider a self-sufficient island with ten men who make their living by fishing from a communal boat. Along comes a new, technologically better way of fishing—for example, using a large net instead of ten individual fishing lines. Now two fishermen, one to pilot the boat and one to throw the net, can catch the same amount of fish as ten fisherman could with lines.

On the surface, unemployment on our hypothetical island has risen from zero to 80 percent, since eight of the ten fisherman are now out of a job. Yet, although eight of the men are no longer working, the society as a whole is still as wealthy, for now two fisherman using the net catch as many fish as ten used to catch using individual lines.

This is exactly what happens every time a machine or technological advance causes a worker to lose his job. In the short term, the society as a whole is just as rich because it still receives the output of the displaced worker's labor (now performed by the machine), and in the long term it will be even richer when the temporarily displaced individ-

---

[4]While the term *Luddite* has come to mean one who is against technological progress, the original Luddites (named after their self-invented mythical leader, King Ludd, of Sherwood Forest) destroyed textile machinery as much to protest wages and working conditions as to protest technological advancements.

ual finds a new job that increases the gross national product.

Now let's go back to our island which has to feed and clothe eight unemployed fishermen. The island society has the option of either taxing the two working fishermen 80 percent and redistributing 80 percent of their fish to the unemployed, or assisting the eight unemployed men in finding new jobs that will add to the wealth of the community. As ludicrous as the former option may sound today, increasing the marginal tax rate to 80 percent (or more) on the producers of society was the primary worldwide response during this century as the implementation of technological advances made certain men far richer than their neighbors.[5]

This type of massive productivity increase (two men doing the work of ten) is what is happening in our Alchemic world today. And the reason this has not led to an increase in unemployment is that, in the alchemic world, where demand is unlimited, we have an insatiable appetite for workers to make *new* goods and provide *new* services.

It is important to realize, however, that many of the jobs found by these workers, like the majority of the high-paying jobs we have today, will be made obsolete tomorrow. For example, if you are a computer programmer, in high demand, you can be sure that new programs will be developed to aid computer programming, as a result of which your company will need fewer programmers to perform the same task. If you are a skilled welder on an assembly line, you can be sure that either robots will be developed to perform your job, or a new manufacturing process will be introduced that will eliminate the need for skilled welding.

Wherever jobs exist, it is only a matter of time before some smart Alchemist finds a way to automate them or increase their productivity so that the demand for them is reduced. When this happens, the goal for society is to get the displaced worker back to work producing something useful as soon as possible. The moment the displaced worker finds such a job, the society as a whole further increases its wealth.

Thus, in the alchemic world, wealth is increased through the elimination of less productive jobs and the creation of new, more productive

[5]By the latter half of the twentieth century the majority of the world, including the United States, either was communist (100 percent taxation) or taxed personal income to the extent that the marginal tax rate (local, state, and federal) was at least 80 percent for income above a certain level.

ones. As technology advances, individual jobs are eliminated; yet the gross national product remains unchanged because society still receives the products or services from those jobs, which are now performed by machine. And when the displaced worker finds a new job that adds to the gross national product, society experiences a dramatic increase in wealth. This is the alchemic process by which our real wealth is increasing at an exponential pace.

The economist Joseph A. Schumpeter has argued that innovation or technological advance is a process of "creative destruction," in which new capital equipment positively displaces older obsolete capital equipment.[6] In our alchemic world, where labor is capital, the worker performing the less productive job can be thought of as the obsolete equipment, and the worker performing the new job can be thought of as the new, more productive equipment. As bad as unemployment may seem to the individual, it is the first step in the alchemic process leading to the creation of real wealth; when the displaced worker finds a new job, we, and one hopes the worker as well, will be richer.

One might think that a worker displaced by automation, when reemployed, will earn more from his or her new job. After all, the old job, by definition, was inefficient, and by accepting the new one he or she adds to the general wealth. However, this is not always the case. A labor department study of 5.1 million workers displaced between 1979 and 1984 showed that, of those who had taken jobs by 1985, nearly one-third had earnings gains of 20 percent or more; but one-fifth had taken pay cuts of 20 percent or more.[7]

The U.S. Labor Department estimates that from 1986 to the year 2000 total U.S. manufacturing employment is projected to decline by approximately 5 percent (834,000 jobs), yet total manufacturing output is projected to rise by 37 percent, paralleling the overall growth in GNP.[8] This means that, even after allowing for a continuing rise in imported manufactured goods, U.S. manufacturers will be producing

[6]Joseph A. Schumpeter, *Capitalism, Socialism, and Democracy* (New York: Harper & Brothers, 1950), 81–87.

[7]Robert J. Samuelson, "The American Job Machine," *Newsweek,* 23 February 1987, 57.

[8]U.S. Department of Labor, Bureau of Labor Statistics, *Projections 2000* (Washington: Government Printing Office, 1988), 30.

approximately 37 percent more real goods with approximately 5 percent fewer workers.

Actually, the government's projected decline of 834,000 manufacturing jobs is misleading, for it does not reflect the true problem. Approximately 10 million, not 834,000, of the present 20 million or so manufacturing jobs will not exist by the end of this century. During this time nearly another 10 million jobs will be created. The Labor Department figure of 834,000 reflects only the *net* change. In human terms, in just the manufacturing sector of our economy, which accounts for approximately 20 percent of total employment, almost half of the people working today—nearly 10 million fathers and mothers whose families depend on their support—will be out of their current jobs by the end of this decade. True, almost another 10 million jobs will be created in the supposedly declining manufacturing sector whose domestic output is expected to rise 37 percent, but the statistics mask the cruel fact that the 10 million people losing their jobs will not necessarily be the same 10 million or so obtaining the new ones.

The broad picture, however, isn't so gloomy. During approximately this same period, when the number of manufacturing jobs is expected to decline by 5 percent, *total* U.S. employment is expected to rise by a whopping 25 percent, despite an expected population increase of only 15 percent.[9] This dramatic increase in total employment will come mostly from new jobs filled by new entrants to the labor force, who primarily will be nonwhite, women, and immigrants (white male employment is expected to grow only 15 percent).[10] But again, this optimistic 25 million net new jobs figure masks the fact that the millions of people who lose their jobs will not necessarily be among the millions of people who obtain the new ones.

This is the alchemic labor dilemma facing us today. Each year in our country, as millions of jobs are permanently lost and even more millions of jobs are created, we are beginning to see an increasing bifurcation in our population. The worker who loses a job is less and less often the worker who finds one. We seem to be creating one class of formerly employed or never-employed workers who lack the skills to take any of

[9] *Workforce 2000—Work and Workers for the Twenty-First Century* (Indianapolis: Hudson Institute, 1987), 96.

[10] *Workforce 2000—Work and Workers for the Twenty-First Century*, 95.

the new jobs, and another class of overemployed workers whose opportunities seem without limit.

Schumpeter argued that innovation, in which less efficient machines are displaced by better ones, is a process of creative destruction. In our alchemic world, where our labor supply is our capital, what we need is a process of *creative reconstruction*—a process to ensure that displaced workers find new, and it is hoped better, jobs.

I once asked my father the difference between a recession and a depression. He told me that in a recession, your next-door neighbor loses his job; in a depression, you lose your job.

We have seen the alchemic explanation of how technological change affects total employment, and how unemployment can occur in a prosperous economy. Let's now examine the labor supply itself under the alchemic microscope to see if we can better understand how, from the individual perspective, one can ensure that the worst one might encounter, as my father would have put it, will be a recession, rather than a depression.

Ten thousand years ago we had no problem matching potential employees and employers. All workers were, more or less, as equal as they were on the day they were born. What has changed to make them so unequal today? Certainly not the worker, since human evolution hasn't changed much in the past ten thousand years. Therefore, it must be the jobs.

The first worker may have been someone hired to pick up the apples that had fallen off the tree in Adam and Eve's garden and put them in a basket. A rather uncomplicated task, easily learned and one requiring no prior experience or knowledge. Then someone may have discovered that the less ripened apples, still hanging on the tree, tasted better and lasted longer once picked. Now the worker had to learn how to climb the tree or use a stick to knock the apples down, as well as to distinguish between the ripened and unripened ones. Still not a difficult task, almost as easily learned and requiring only the knowledge of his prior job.

Then one day someone may have decided to promote the worker and send him to another land to plant apple trees. Now this was difficult. In addition to mastering the requirements of his prior job, the worker had to be trained to obtain the seeds, select a place to plant them, determine the best time of the year to plant, and care for the seedlings until the trees were old enough to survive on their own. Most important, there was so much information to remember, over such a long period of time, that the worker probably had to write it down so as not to forget it. In other words, he had to have mastered what today we call a basic skill—writing—in order to advance to his new position.

This is what is happening in our alchemic world today. We are all getting promoted. All of our jobs are being upgraded in terms of their contribution to society, and the upgraded positions are increasingly dependent on our having what we call *basic skills*— skills not currently taught in the workplace, which we are presumed to have mastered before beginning to work.

The definition of basic skills typically used by employers includes the ability to read and write, perform mathematical computations, communicate (verbally and in writing), and solve problems. Simply stated, our basic skills are our ability to read, write, calculate, speak, listen, and reason.[11] Just as the speed with which our society processes information is the throttle on the overall advance of technology, the speed with which we process or learn new information, which is controlled by the level of our basic skills, is the throttle on the overall advance of our individual abilities.

Thus, success in most of our jobs today is, and in virtually all of our jobs tomorrow will be, determined less by mastering the specific task we perform and more by thoroughly mastering the basic skills. This is because in our dynamic alchemic economy the task that we perform today will be technologically obsolete tomorrow. The new method we will learn tomorrow will probably be such a technological improvement over the old one that the speed with which we implement it will likely be more important than how well we perform it.

For example, suppose you work in an office where your work output, be it as a lawyer, a paper processor, or even a manager, is dependent on your ability to write and edit documents. Along comes a new word-processing system that, with all its new formatting features, can double the speed with which you produce your documentation, greatly

[11]Note that the definition of *basic skills* does not include such things as keen eyesight, good health, etc., as medical advances have made them so ubiquitous that they are no longer major criteria in the hiring process. For example, before corrective lenses were readily available, good eyesight was probably a key factor in employment decisions.

improving your productivity. If your basic skills are the highest in your department, you will probably be the first one to learn the new system, thereby increasing your productivity first while the others catch up. By the time your co-workers master the new technology, there will likely be an even better system available, starting the whole process all over again.

The ability to learn new methods and skills is a key determinant of productivity in the factory or shop as well as in the office. Suppose you're an automobile mechanic. Until recently, the more experience you had diagnosing and correcting problems, the better and more efficient you became at your job as the same problems occurred over and over again. But not anymore. All the experience you had fixing carburetors went out the window in the 1980s with the advent of the fuel injector. And your experience repairing mechanical speedometers is becoming obsolete as instrument panels become electronic.

In today's alchemic environment, where significant advances in automobile technology are made every year, it is difficult for mechanics to keep abreast of new technology—air bags, electronic pollution control equipment, computerized braking systems, and the like. Therefore, the best auto mechanic is the one who can read and understand the yearly repair manuals the fastest, best communicate the problem to the factory, determine the logical solution, and service or repair the car. The specific or *functional* knowledge gained from twenty years' experience as an auto mechanic is mostly valuable today only to the extent that it adds to the mechanic's *generic* knowledge or basic skill level, thereby enhancing his or her overall ability to learn.

Most of us think we are learning a valuable skill or trade when we start a new job. We are, but it's usually valuable only for a short period of time. What we accomplish of lasting value when we master a new job is the increase in our basic skill level and in our confidence in our ability to learn something new.

An alchemic employer looking at a résumé today is as interested in the applicant's basic skill level as in his or her specific functional abilities. First, there are literally tens of thousands of different job descriptions in our alchemic economy, with hundreds being added and subtracted each year, making it more and more difficult for an employer to match a needed skill with a prospective employee. Moreover, alchemic employers know that a prospective employee's ability to learn the new job functions that will be coming along tomorrow is as important as, if not more important than, his or her existing ability to perform a specific task. Therefore, alchemic employers focus increasingly on generic rather than functional knowledge—that is, the potential employee's basic skill level which determines his or her speed at learning specific skills—as the key determinant in the hiring process.

An employee's basic skills and the job function he or she performs are analogous to the hardware and software in a personal computer. A computer's hardware can have varying amounts of core memory, ranging today from sixty-four kilobytes to sixteen megabytes. But regardless of its core memory, a computer can't do anything without software, which is constantly being upgraded with new versions that usually require more memory. The objective for the computer owner is to purchase enough memory to run the software that will become available over the expected life of the machine, or at least ensure that memory capacity can be upgraded as needed.

Today, alchemic employers recognize that to stay in business they must constantly retrain their workers, upgrading their functional skills to match the requirements of the changing jobs they perform. However, as more and more new jobs are developed which require a higher level of basic skills, employers must either increase their existing employees' level of basic skills or hire new employees who have such skills. Unfortunately, most employers today usually find it faster and less expensive to choose the latter option.

An employer who wants to help his or her employees upgrade their basic skills would likely find it a marginal proposition, for several reasons. First, money spent on upgrading an employee's basic skills may not yield a return for several years. Second, the employer may not be the direct beneficiary of the investment. In today's dynamic employment market, there is no guarantee that the employee won't leave and take his or her enhanced skills elsewhere. And finally, accounting regulations in the United States provide more advantages for investment in new equipment than for investment in human beings.[12]

So what should an employee do, knowing that the job or function

[12]Under Generally Accepted Accounting Principles, investments in physical capital are amortized over the expected life of the physical item, while investments in human capital are expensed because there is no guarantee that the return from the money expended (on human capital) will be realized by the company incurring the expense.

106

he or she is being paid to perform today will be obsolete tomorrow? The answer is to improve the hardware (increase his or her level of basic skills) rather than improve the software (get better and better at performing his or her particular job).

This is more easily said than done, because we are not presently well equipped to handle the adult member of our society who wants to upgrade his or her level of basic skills. However, as we shall see, we will have to become so equipped in the very near future. This is not just because we may want to serve the worker displaced by automation, or because we may want to provide additional opportunities for the employee who wants to get ahead. Although these are noble social goals, *we are going to have to find a way to upgrade the basic skills of our adult population, because for the past two decades our educational system has dismally failed approximately one-fourth of our citizens, graduating tens of millions of functionally illiterate high school students who are ill-equipped to become productive members of our society.*

EDUCATION

Real improvement, everyone now agrees, will require nothing less than a complete restructuring of U.S. schools.[1]

IN THE PAST, a productive resource of society was typically located near its most important capital source, be it the farm on arable land, the gristmill on the river, or the steel mill near the coal and iron supply. This is still true. Today, however, the most important capital source in our alchemic world—where physical resources are far less important than technological ones—is the supply of labor. And the labor supply increasingly means the *educated* labor supply.

Thus in a cover story on the best cities for businesses seeking to relocate, *Fortune* reported that the "first and most important" criterion in selecting a site is the availability of an appropriately educated labor force.[2]

The *Fortune* story explained what made each of the top-ten cities on its list the best. For example, in Dallas, "the business community has played a crucial role in uplifting education"; in Los Angeles, the "vast labor pool has helped make Los Angeles a mecca for the apparel

[1]Nancy J. Perry, "How to Help America's Schools," *Fortune*, 4 December 1989, 138.

[2]"The Best Cities For Business," *Fortune*, 23 October 1989, 56.

industry"; and in Portland, "the living environment has attracted the well-educated and well-skilled."[3] But none of the ten cities really excelled in attracting or training educated workers; they simply were not as bad as the rest.

The cold, hard fact is that despite all our alchemic success stories, the U.S. public educational system has failed all but its upper-class citizens, and the exception for the upper class is only because they have abandoned it. In a recent survey, 25 percent of young adults in Dallas, the number-one city on *Fortune's* list, "couldn't identify the country that borders the United States to the south."[4] Of the approximately 2.4 million citizens in the United States who graduate from high school each year, approximately one-quarter—600,000—"cannot read and write at the eighth grade 'functionally literate' level," and that dismal figure doesn't include another *"one million* young people who drop out of high school every year" before graduation.[5]

When Thomas Jefferson wrote that all men are created equal, he meant that they were basically born equal and were to be given equal opportunity to remain so. But when we perpetuate an educational system that practically destroys all opportunities for 1.6 million young Americans each year, we are not giving them equal opportunity to compete, or even function, in our society. Moreover, of the 2.4 million who do not drop out, "Most 17-year-olds in school cannot summarize a newspaper article, write a good letter requesting a job, solve real-life math problems, or follow a bus schedule."[6]

In the late nineteenth century, the U.S. educational system was the envy of the world. When a group of British industrialists set sail in 1851 to investigate why the United States was second to England in industry and catching up fast, they found that "American manufacturing prowess is in large part due to a highly educated work force. The Yankees have an astonishingly high literacy rate of 90% among the free population. In the industrial heartland of New England 95% of adults read

[3]"The Best Cities For Business," 58–70.

[4]David T. Kearns, "David T. Kearns," *Harvard Business Review*, November-December 1988, 70.

[5]"America's Schools Still Aren't Making the Grade," *Business Week*, 19 September 1988, 129 (emphasis added).

[6]"America's Schools Still Aren't Making the Grade," 129.

and write. In contrast, just two-thirds of the people in Britain are literate."[7]

What happened? How did we go from having the best educational system to the worst? Before we answer that question, let's examine some of the many areas in which we have come to excel over the same period.

First, transportation. The United States has the best transportation system in the world for both people and goods. Despite the great distance, it costs an American far less to travel, or ship a product, from New York to California than it does his European counterpart to travel or ship a fraction of that distance.

Second, retailing. The United States today has approximately 1.5 million retail stores selling hundreds of thousands of different types of goods. The U.S. system of distributing goods from the factory to the consumer is the best in the free world by a wide margin, and a major contributor to our world economic power status.

Third, food service. The United States today has approximately 400,000 restaurants offering so many varieties of food, and such a wide range of prices, that Americans eat almost half their meals outside of the home. U.S. restaurant concepts are so popular that they can be found in virtually every corner of the globe, from Kentucky Fried Chicken in Tokyo to McDonald's in Moscow.

The list goes on and on. In so many areas of importance to our life-styles, the United States is second to none.[8] So why should our public education system, to which we entrust our children and our future, be such a failure? The answer lies in the alchemic understanding of how the United States developed so well in so many areas *but* public education.

In transportation, retailing, and food service, as well as in virtually every other successful area of our economy, we have seen massive productivity growth through the advance of technology. Today's cars, department stores, and fast-food outlets have come a long way from the

[7]"America's Schools Still Aren't Making the Grade," 100–101.

[8]Obviously, there are many areas that the United States lags disgracefully behind other developed nations, such as the average level of health care; as we shall see later on, this is primarily a function of the fact that many of our citizens are being left behind in our alchemic prosperity.

horse and buggy, the general store, and the Main Street soda shop. In fact, these industries have evolved so fast technologically that we have seen them change before our eyes.

In Chapter 4 we saw how the technology gap—the best production practice possible with current knowledge versus the practice in actual use—is the determinant of technological, and thus economic, growth. However, we didn't explore *why* someone would want to discover, and then implement, a better way of doing something. How many of us continually research whether our present method of doing something is technologically obsolete, and, upon discovering that it is, make time to learn the new method? The answer is, very few.

For most of us, life seems filled to capacity. There isn't time to learn something new, or even find out what is new that we should learn. Even when we know that our lives could be easier, better, or more productive by implementing a new method of doing something, we generally do so only when we know that we will be either out of a job or out of business if we don't. But if most of us aren't inclined to learn something new, why are there so many new things to learn? What drives all this innovation?

The constant innovation in our society is driven by the few among us who discover and implement technological gaps—our true, modern-day Alchemists. The universal trait among successful entrepreneurs today is the belief, like that held by the ancient alchemist in his quest to make gold out of base metals, that there is a better way out there, and that by finding and using it they can reap great financial rewards for themselves and for their society. While some of these entrepreneurs are motivated by the thrill of discovery or the resultant fame, it is primarily financial reward that drives them. Even when they become so wealthy that financial rewards have relatively little value, money still serves as a scorecard, the scale on which they can measure society's need and appreciation for what they do.

This process of innovation and implementation has been driving the exponential advance of technology in our society. It starts with the entrepreneur—our modern-day Alchemist—who believes that he or she can discover and help us implement a new and better way of doing something. It ends with the rest of us—too busy with our personal lives or not driven enough to be the entrepreneur—who implement the new and better way, knowing that if we don't our employer or our customer will find another employee or supplier who will.

This is the process that Schumpeter has argued accounts for the economic strength of capitalism over any comparative system, the "creative destruction" process whereby each provider of a good or service is constantly forced by competition to "incessantly revolutionize" from "within, incessantly destroying the old" structure and "incessantly creating a new one."[9] This process of constant technological advance is what drives our capitalist economy in every area but one.

This one area, of course, is public education. And the reason it has been left out is that we have been trying to apply an economic solution to the problem rather than an alchemic one.

When we needed more railroads to transport more people and materials across our nation, we didn't simply pay more to the nineteenth-century railroad barons for more service. Rather, the free market forced the transportation system to innovate, leading to the development of a dynamic system that continually optimizes the use of available highways, airports, harbors, and rail terminals for each community and providing for each industry a continually changing array of motor vehicles, planes, ships, and trains.

Similarly, our diversified retailing industry didn't grow because we simply paid more to the owners of the general stores to expand. Rather, the free market forced the system to innovate, leading to the creation of a changing mix of shopping centers, mail-order businesses, mass-merchandisers, specialty stores, and new types of merchandising techniques that greatly improved the distribution of our merchandise from manufacturer to consumer.

And our food service industry didn't grow to over 400,000 successful restaurants because we simply paid the owners to expand their current operations. The free market forced the system to innovate, leading to the construction of fast-food outlets and gourmet restaurants in virtually every community in America, with new menus, new restaurants, and new concepts evolving on almost a daily basis.

And yet, during the many years that we have been hearing about our crisis in education, we have responded by increasing the amount paid to already-failing teachers and administrators, effectively saying "Let's

---

[9]Joseph A. Schumpeter, *Capitalism, Socialism, and Democracy,* (New York: Harper and Brothers, 1950), 83.

pay more money to the same people to continue to do the same thing." As a result of this response—increasing the payment for duration rather than innovation—today there is little correlation between the amount of money spent on public education and the quantity or quality of the results.

For example, in the state of New Jersey, where public education expenditures average approximately $7,571 per student per year, a child receives a $90,000 primary and secondary education from public funds. By contrast, in the state of Utah, where public education expenditures average approximately $2,571 per student per year, a child receives a $30,000 primary and secondary education from public funds.[10] And yet, as unbelievable as it may seem, despite this vast 300 percent difference in cost, the average education received by a public school student in Utah is actually *superior* to that of a public school student in New Jersey. The high school graduation percentage in Utah is higher than it is in New Jersey (80.6 percent as opposed to 77.2 percent), and the composite average SAT scores for Utah are considerably higher than the composite average SAT scores for New Jersey (1034 contrasted to 893).

Since 1960, spending per child in U.S. public schools has risen 300 percent, but standardized test results have plummeted; for example, average SAT scores have declined approximately 100 points.[11] More important, during the 1980s, despite a dramatic increase in per-pupil expenditures, there was little or no change in the percentage of young adults graduating from high school. In New York State, from roughly 1982 to 1987, despite a 51 percent increase in per-pupil expenditures ($4,825 to $7,338), the percentage of high school graduates actually fell slightly, from 63.4 to 62.9. In Michigan, per-pupil expenditures during this same period increased more than 30 percent (from $3,498 to $4,576), while the percentage of high school graduates fell, from 71.6 to 62.4. And in Massachusetts, where per-pupil expenditures rose an astronomical 83 percent, the percentage of high school graduates remained virtually unchanged. Nationwide, as in these individual states,

[10]This figure results from multiplying by twelve years the annual expenditures of education of $7,571 and $2,574 for New Jersey and Utah, respectively. From "State of the States," *American School Board Journal,* 176, no. 10 (October 1989).

[11]Perry, "How to Help America's Schools," 138.

there seems to be little or no correlation between the amount of money spent on public education and the quantity or quality of students graduating from high school. Between 1983 and 1988, per-pupil expenditures in the United States rose 42 percent, with little change in the percentage of high school graduates.[12]

Yet, despite a documented low correlation between money spent and improvement in the quantity and quality of public education, the reform of public education has focused almost exclusively on the financial issue. In October 1989, the Texas Supreme Court ruled that the state's system of funding public education through local property tax revenues was unconstitutional because it resulted in vast discrepancies in the amounts spent on individual children.[13] To the Texas Supreme Court, it is a denial of individual civil rights to grant one child a $30,000 education with public funds while granting another child a $90,000 education with public funds, just because the two children happen to reside in different school districts. And yet while this is a positive step forward for individual human rights in maintaining equal opportunity for all Texas citizens, it still ignores the fundamental reason that our educational industry has not kept pace with the rest of the economy, namely a lack of innovation. In this age of the computer and the automobile, we are still attempting to teach our children using educational methods that were mostly developed in, and little removed from, the age of the quill pen and the horsedrawn carriage.

The reason that there has been little or no innovation in education is that there has been little or no competition to stimulate and reward it. This is not readily apparent, because in the absence of competition it is often difficult to perceive that there is a way of doing something better than the way in which it is already being done. And yet once we examine our educational industry in this light, the problem becomes as obvious as was Galileo's observation that the earth orbits the sun. Like Galileo, we need only discard our prejudices and open our minds to view the subject from a fresh perspective.

For example, our present 180-day school year, with classes ending in mid-afternoon and a long summer recess, was designed for a

12"State of the States."

13Paul Zane Pilzer, "Free Choice Could Be Cornerstone of New Texas School System," *Dallas Morning News*, 6 October 1989, 25A.

nineteenth-century agrarian economy where children were needed at home to help with chores and harvesting. Yet today, more than half a century after the conversion of our agrarian civilization to an urban one, we still haven't changed the school calendar to conform to our modern requirements. If something as obvious as the calendar itself hasn't changed for over a hundred years, think what our classrooms, teaching methods, and textbooks must still be like.

When I was a teaching assistant at the Wharton Graduate Business School in 1975, certain courses were taught with a computer program that we referred to as a "three-dimensional interactive textbook," an innovation we thought would revolutionize the entire educational industry by the end of the decade. The 3-D interactive textbook was a computerized teaching program that allowed students to read a textbook, page by page, on their monitors. The computer would periodically ask questions to determine the students' comprehension of the material presented. If the program determined that a student needed extra help with a particular subject, it would present additional material on that subject before proceeding to the next lesson.

For example, an economics course taught with such a system might contain a lesson about the Federal Reserve Bank. Before going into an in-depth explanation of the Federal Reserve, the computer would ask the student if he or she already knew about this subject. If the student answered yes, the computer would ask a few questions to confirm that knowledge and then advance to the next lesson. If the student answered no, the computer would present the lesson on the Federal Reserve and then query the student to see if he or she understood it. If the student failed the query, the computer would present one or more in-depth lessons on the subject—the "third dimension" of the program—until the student could successfully give responses demonstrating mastery of the material. Thus every student could learn at his or her own pace without the slower students holding up the faster ones and without the faster students embarrassing the slower ones. At the end of the class, the computer gave the teaching assistants a report showing how the class was doing as a whole and which students needed additional help or time with their lessons.

As teachers, we were enthralled with the three-dimensional interactive textbook because we saw its potential effect on education. Once this product was installed in our schools, students would have the opportunity to learn every subject from the most knowledgeable minds in each field, since these people could be hired to write the three-dimensional program for his or her field of expertise. But our dreams have not been realized, and the reason is due neither to cost nor technology. In 1975, the hardware for each classroom, a relatively simple main computer attached to thirty or so terminals, cost less than 10 percent of the amount we were unsuccessfully spending each year to educate each child. And today, fifteen years later, its cost has fallen considerably. But such a system is still far from being implemented. And meanwhile, as the teachers and administrators in our schools failed to take full advantage of the opportunities presented by such new technological advances, the computer industry put Pac-Man and its successors in every convenience store and shopping center, and successfully marketed a Nintendo or Atari video game to every U.S. household with children. As a result, U.S. children have come to view computer technology as something more for recreation and entertainment than for education.

The public education industry has approximately 4.3 million highly dedicated employees[14] who sincerely care about the welfare of their students. Each year these dedicated professionals put in longer and longer hours for less and less pay (relative to other professions), only to fail in their efforts to give 1.6 million young people the minimal level of skills that society requires as the ticket of admission to a productive life. They, like their students, are trapped; they are like Sisyphus, the mythical Greek character who was condemned forever to push a rock up a hill, only to have it roll down each time it almost reached the top.

These teachers, like their students, have become cogs in a perpetual failure machine. They have been given a task to perform but have not been given the tools and incentives required to perform it. This is analogous to having asked the great pyramid builders of ancient Egypt to build a modern-day skyscraper; regardless of their skill and their level of commitment to the project, they simply wouldn't have had the requisite technology or the materials to succeed.

By contrast, we *do* know how to build a productive school system.

[14]Approximately 2.3 million teachers, 600,000 instructional staff members, and 1.4 million nonprofessional staff. From U.S. Department of Education, National Center for Education Statistics, *Digest of Education Statistics 1989* (Washington: Government Printing Office, 1989), 83.

This is evidenced by the 12 percent of the students in the United States—approximately 5.7 million out of 45.7 million—who attend private schools.[15] Virtually all of these students graduate from high school with basic skills far above the national average. (Although this is partially because they attract a more prepared student in the first place, few would doubt that the same student would perform better in a private school environment than in a public one.)

In order to get the public education industry on the alchemic train of technological advances that the rest of our economy, and many of our private school systems, have been enjoying for decades, we must institute a freely competitive system in which our educators have incentives to create and implement innovative techniques. Only through the process of creative destruction—the process that has made the U.S. economy the most productive per employee in the world—can we get a continual process of innovation incorporated into our public schools. This may or may not require the complete demolition of our existing state-managed public educational system, a system which provides little incentive for the individual teacher or administrator to innovate. But after years of trying countless ineffectual solutions, it may be that, as *Fortune* magazine recently put it, "Real improvement . . . will require nothing less that a complete restructuring of U.S. schools."[16]

Here's how we can restructure the public education industry to implement the alchemic process of innovation through creative destruction in our schools.

The approximately $5,000 per-pupil per year—$292 billion overall— that we currently spend on public education would be given to the parents of each child in the form of a tuition certificate. The certificate could be presented to any accredited public or private school selected by the parents to educate their child. The school would be able to redeem the tuition certificate for an amount between $2,500 and $7,500, depending on how much the student learned that year relative to the average learned by all students in the system (that is, the total cost would still average $5,000 per student per year).

[15]U.S. Department of Commerce, Bureau of the Census, *Statistical Abstract of the United States 1989* (Washington: Government Printing Office, 1989), 124.

[16]Perry, "How to Help America's Schools," 138.

The authorities currently responsible for overseeing the educational process would remain in business, but would function in a regulatory role analogous to that of public health officials. For example, a restaurant, in order to stay in business, must periodically qualify for a certificate from the local board of health. Similarly, each school, in order to redeem the variable tuition certificate, would have to meet the minimum standards of federal, state, and local authorities.

During the first year of such a system it is likely that the existing public school districts would still be the major providers of educational services. But here's what would eventually happen in every community.

The best teachers and principals would band together and form new schools, perhaps led by businesspeople and other professionals seeking to make their fortunes by doing a better job educating America's youth. This new $292 billion industry, as the largest in the United States (nearly six times the size of the U.S. automobile manufacturing industry),[17] would clearly attract our best and brightest Alchemists.

Local authorities would be able to maintain publicly owned and operated schools, but only if these schools could successfully compete with the new private and public schools in their areas. If a school was closed because it couldn't compete, entrepreneurs would flock to lease or purchase the building and open a new school in its place. As education became a profitable business, entrepreneurs would also design and build new innovative school facilities.

Public and private companies would work with the schools and municipalities to provide transportation for each student over the widest possible area, thereby expanding the number of schools available to each student.

All parents would have the opportunity that wealthy Americans have always enjoyed—the ability to choose the best school for their child regardless of their income. Now, for the first time in history, all 45.7 million U.S. schoolchildren, not just the 5.7 million privileged ones in private schools today, would be given the equal opportunity envisioned by Thomas Jefferson in the Declaration of Independence.

However, the real excitement would be provided by the variable

[17]In 1987 the U.S. automobile manufacturing industry was estimated as having approximately $50 billion in sales. This contrasts with a $36 billion hotel industry, a $223 billion health services industry, and a $10.7 billion motion picture industry. *Statistical Abstract of the United States 1989,* 422.

feature of the tuition certificate. Students would be tested at the beginning of each school year to determine what they already knew. The testing would be conducted by public authorities or by a private firm hired to perform this important service. Then the students would be retested at the end of the school year and the school would be paid an amount, ranging from $2,500 to $7,500 per student, based on how much the individual students had learned.

Special certificates, probably paying considerably higher amounts, would be available for students with learning disabilities or with demographic profiles suggesting that they learned at a slower pace than others. These special certificates, paying above-average amounts, would provide an economic incentive for private entrepreneurs to accept students with special needs into their schools, or to develop separate schools or programs tailored to meet their special needs.

Competition would be intense among the best and the brightest individuals, both inside and outside of schools, to develop innovative methods for teaching every subject. Top corporations such as General Electric and IBM, which can afford to commit massive sums to researching and developing new educational methods, would emerge as service providers to, and managers of, entrepreneurially operated schools. Outstanding teachers would be recruited, in the same manner as top corporate executives, to teach students as well as potential teachers. Writers of the best textbooks and designers of the best teaching methods would come to be regarded as top inventors as each school, and each service provider to the schools, sought to be on the cutting edge of new technological advances.

Education would become what it used to be—the most respected of all the professions—only now for the first time teachers would have the opportunity to be compensated according to their performance.

Although this concept may seem radical, our current educational system is so bad that we have very little to lose. We can and must develop a new system that will attract and reward those who successfully create and implement innovation in our public schools. Such a new system will only work if it recognizes the fact that increasing innovation, rather than increasing compensation, is what we need to reform the public educational industry in our alchemic world.

During the 1980s, "no pass—no play" was an educational issue that dominated the media. It referred to a Texas state law requiring students to pass a minimum number of courses in order to participate in sports. Unfortunately, the policy focused on the symptom of the problem—unmotivated students—rather than the disease itself—an educational system that failed to encourage and reward innovative methods of motivating students. Perhaps the concept of "no pass—no play," which was applied to the students, would have been much more effective if it had been "no pass—no *pay*," and applied to the teachers and administrators.

CHILDREN

And the Lord said unto Cain: "Where is Abel thy brother?" And he said:
"I know not; am I my brother's keeper?"

—Genesis 4:9

SOME PEOPLE CLAIM that there is nothing wrong with the U.S. system
of public education itself. They claim that the problem lies with minority students who have difficulty learning, and that our educational
system is failing only because we are comparing the abilities of minority
students to the abilities of nonminorities who are able to learn faster.
But the facts demonstrate that this is merely an attempt by some
members of the public educational establishment to shift the blame
from themselves.

The state of Texas conducts a Texas Educational Assessment of
Minimum Skills (TEAMS) test to measure student performance in
grades one through eleven. In 1989, over 70 percent of white ninth-grade students passed the ninth-grade TEAMS tests, while only 46 and
49 percent of black and Hispanic students, respectively, passed the test.
Yet, among first-graders, whose parents and home life are obviously the
predominant influence on their performance, 70 percent of black and
Hispanic students passed the TEAMS tests.[1] This led a recent report

[1] *Report Card on Texas Schools* (Dallas: National Center for Policy Analysis,
1990), 6..

121

on Texas schools to conclude that "the more time students spend in school, the greater the performance gap between white and minority students."[2] As the president of the organization sponsoring the report recently wrote, "Minority children are not the cause of the failure of the public schools, they are the most tragic victims of that failure."[3]

Although most children may be born roughly equal, they are no longer so by the time they enter public school. Irrespective of minority status, children from low-income families perform significantly worse when they begin public education than do children from more privileged economic backgrounds.[4] It is now well recognized that certain students entering public schools perform considerably better if they are given a head start, which, in fact, was the name of a widely implemented and successful preschool program in the 1960s to give children of poorer families an equal place at the starting line when they began regular public education.

Project Head Start, which in practice resembles a nursery school, was founded in 1965 to serve the developmental needs of handicapped children and children from low-income families. Head Start is considered one of the few successes in our educational industry because it has helped get millions of young, potentially disadvantaged Americans onto the educational road to success. Yet the true Alchemist, who is always looking to what can be, rather than what is, would consider it a dismal failure because its approximately 448,000 current participants represents only 22 percent of the more than 2 million legally eligible children who should be reaping its benefits.[5] Moreover, this figure of 2 million legally eligible children represents only the number eligible because of their low-income or handicapped status, not the millions more who could benefit from such a program but are deemed ineligible because they are not disadvantaged enough.

Historically, we didn't need programs like Project Head Start for disadvantaged children because society accepted the responsibility for raising every child to achieve his or her potential. Until approximately

[2]Report Card on Texas Schools, 3.

[3]John C. Goodman, "How to Improve Education," Dallas Morning News, 8 February 1990, 19A.

[4]Report Card on Texas Schools.

[5]Digest of Education Statistics 1989, (Washington: Government Printing Office, 1989), 356.

ten thousand years ago the dominant form of food production was hunting animals and the gathering of wild plants. Humankind lived in migratory tribes that collectively took responsibility for raising their children. An abundant supply of food was available, provided you had the capital—the people—to hunt and gather it. And as the society became more efficient through the division and specialization of individual labor, each person trained to hunt or gather added more to the tribal welfare than he or she consumed. Individual wealth was increased by increasing tribal wealth, and tribal wealth was increased by ensuring that every member of the tribe maximized his or her potential. Tribal ritual guaranteed that each child was brought up to be a fully functioning member of the society with the collective values of the tribe, regardless of the status or ability of his or her parents. The tribe, acting in its own best interests, assumed collective responsibility for raising the next generation.

Then approximately ten thousand years ago, with the development of agriculture, the technology of food production changed. For the first time, people could effectively control their food production as the economically productive unit shifted from the much larger migratory tribe, involved in hunting and gathering, to the much smaller stationary farm family, involved in cultivation.

The agrarian society had a different social agenda when it came to raising the next generation. In contrast to the tribe, which increased its wealth by increasing the productivity of all tribal members, the self-sufficient family farmer only benefited from maximizing the potential of the children, usually his own, actually working on his farm. There seemed to be a fixed supply of scarce resources—mainly the land encompassing the farm—and an ever-increasing number of people outside the farm wanting to share them. Thus, unlike the hunter-gatherer, the family farmer had little economic incentive to raise children other than his own.[6]

In contrast to this agrarian model of the farm family with seemingly

---

[6]It should be noted that the agrarian farm family was not the simple mom-dad-and-two-kids family unit we think of today. Parents, children, grandparents, uncles, aunts and cousins all lived and worked together on the family farm in a large extended family. In fact, from a child-raising model, the very large extended family probably didn't differ much from that of the communal hunter-gatherer. But by the beginning of the industrial revolution the extended family unit had been substantially displaced by the immediate family unit we know today.

scarce resources, our alchemic world today is much more like that of the tribal hunter-gatherer, but one with unlimited food to harvest. Today we need more productive people to harvest our resources, since each productive person adds far more to the gross national product than he or she consumes in physical resources.

As we saw in Chapter 3, nearly 95 percent of the U.S. economy is alchemic—involved in the production of goods and services above basic needs—and the potential demand curve for the next few decades seems to be a nearly vertical line into infinite space. In our resource-laden, demand-driven world, our production level of goods and services is determined by our virtually unlimited demand for them.

Today everyone has a vested economic interest in seeing that every child has the opportunity to maximize his or her potential. And yet to many people this is not as obvious as it should be. After all, most of us have been brought up to view our lives in the context of a resource-scarce environment, where the person you train today may be the one who takes your job away tomorrow. However, not only is the person you train today not going to take your job away tomorrow, he or she is probably going to save it by becoming your best customer or your best supplier.

Although today our economic self-interest is best served by our being collectively responsible for all of society's children, our current social structure, which evolved from the self-sufficient family farm, is not designed to accomplish this objective. In fact, for the purpose of assisting all children in reaching their potential, it is far inferior to the tribal communal child-raising model that preceded it, for the following reasons.

First, most parents are inexperienced and frequently incapable of recognizing when a child may have a special need. Parents can benefit from access to a communal brain trust that effectively replaces the extended family to assist them in raising their children. Second, sometimes parents only know that something is wrong with their child when they can observe him or her among the child's peers. Lastly, communal child-rearing is not only potentially better for the child, but for the mother as well. A small child requires an adult supervisor twenty-four hours a day, but two small children together do not require two adult supervisors. In fact, the scale moves in the opposite direction. While one mother can barely supervise one small child, two mothers can supervise up to six small children, three mothers can supervise up to twelve, and so on. This is because the children begin to amuse and take care of each other, and the mothers can efficiently divide their labors.

Thus, in our shift from a tribal to an agrarian society, while the technology of food production may have advanced, the technology of raising children may have taken a step in the opposite direction.

Moreover, a new problem is emerging in the raising of preschool children, to which the problem of rearing more productive children pales by comparison. This problem is one of values—and it is threatening more than just the success of our public educational system; it is threatening the very fabric of our society. Simply stated, far too many of our children are being raised without a sense of the basic, common values that have enabled people to function together and survive as a society. On a basic level, our values are what cause us to go out and work for our primary needs, rather than steal things from someone else who has them. On a higher level, our values are what give meaning to the things that make life worth living, the things that we want once we are no longer striving to satisfy our primary needs.

One of my students once complained to me that life seemed meaningless. I agreed. Life, I told him, as we define it biologically, *is* meaningless; that's why we have invented, if you will, our values—to give life meaning.

This student's lament is indicative of society's failure to instill a sense of values in our young. And the price of this failure is far more than a few disillusioned college students. Consider these facts: there are more black men in the United States today in prison than there are enrolled in four-year colleges;[7] fully 60 percent of daughters of single women on welfare for ten years or more end up on welfare themselves;[8] and from just 1970 to 1986 the number of children born to white unmarried mothers almost tripled, from 50,000 to 138,000 per year.[9]

These dismal reflections of our society are a direct result of the

[7] *To Secure Our Future—The Federal Role in Education* (Rochester, NY: National Center on Education and the Economy, 1989), 12.

[8] "Why the Underclass Can't Get Out From Under," *Business Week,* 19 September 1988, 124.

[9] In 1970, 5.7 percent of all white births were by unmarried women versus 15.7 percent of all white births in 1986. Data from *Statistical Abstract of the United States 1989,* 66.

wholesale breakdown in conveying values to our young. And the problem becomes particularly evident in our first-grade classes, where we ask our teachers to try to teach basic skills to children who have no foundation on which to build. These young children, lacking a sense of basic, common values, are unable to begin learning how to become productive members of society.

We offer many reasons for our failure to instill a sense of values in our young. For example, it is pointed out that in the United States from 1970 to 1987 the percentage of children under eighteen living in a household with no male head nearly doubled, from 10.8 percent to 21.3 percent.[10] It is also noted that more than half of young mothers with children work outside of the home, and that more than a quarter of young mothers are now rearing their children alone. But no one is dealing with the *real* problem: the millions of children who, through no fault of their own, are growing up without a basic sense of values on which the public educational system can build.

Society's focus on this problem has traditionally been in terms of social responsibility, rather than economic opportunity.[11] For example, statistics frequently cite the cost of supporting a person in prison or on welfare, rather than the amount society loses because the prisoner or welfare recipient is not productively contributing to the economy. A man who serves ten years of his life in prison will cost society $216,240 just for the cost of his incarceration,[12] but that same man earning an annual salary of $15,000 would, over a forty-five-year working life, contribute $675,000 to the gross national product.

Our failure to encourage values in our children hinders their ability to learn the basic skills requisite to success in our society. And those children who grow up without these necessary skills are those most likely to end up taking from society rather than contributing to it. Moreover, society loses not only what it costs to support these people

[10]Although the black female heads of households received the most attention during this period (1970–1987), the increase for white Americans (106 percent) was considerably higher than for black Americans (71 percent). Data from *Statistical Abstract of the United States 1989*, 52.

[11]If the focus had been reversed, the problem might have been better highlighted and more might have been done to solve it.

[12]It costs the federal government $21,624 in corrections expenses per year for each federal prisoner. *Statistical Abstract of the United States 1989*, 176, 183.

but the benefits that could have been reaped had these people realized their potential—if not as scientists, engineers, or doctors at least as functioning members of the work force.

Although programs like Project Head Start are laudable and of significant value, it is not enough to merely try to bring our young to an equal place at the starting gate. We must see that all children receive the necessary preschool advantages, in both education and values, in an environment that will help to maximize their individual potential. For unusual though it may seem, we all benefit when the office worker who would have earned $15,000 per year earns $30,000, or when the engineer who would have earned $50,000 per year earns $150,000. In fact, we all benefit when the entrepreneur who would have earned $3 million per year earns $6 million. In the alchemic economy, where one person's gain is *not* another person's loss, we all benefit when anyone increases his or her earnings by becoming more productive.

Above all, we must reorient our focus. We have been directing our attention to the parents, rather than to the children. We have noted certain demographic changes in our society (for example, the increased numbers of divorced parents, female heads-of-households, and working mothers), and have blamed them for the failings of our children. True, addressing these sociological changes would help, but would not get to the root of the problem. We must focus our attention on the fact that too many of our children are being raised without the skills and values required for success in our society, and we must direct our efforts toward changing this situation.

Our educational system presently is failing 47 percent of our youth.[13] In our alchemic world, where labor is capital, no business or society can afford to waste nearly half of its capital. The problem is especially tragic because we have the technology and the resources to prevent it by reforming preschool and public education to maximize the potential of every child.

The alchemic solution to this problem is a national child-care certificate program for preschool children, modeled on the tuition-certificate program for public education described in Chapter 6. It is

---

[13]As noted in Chapter 6, of the 3.4 million potential high school graduates in the United States each year, 1 million drop out and 600,000 of the 2.4 million who do graduate are functionally illiterate.

important to realize that this is a program for *child* care and not day care. Day care is designed to serve the employed parent, the adult individual who wants or needs to work and requires a place to put the child while he or she is on the job. Child care, on the other hand, is designed to serve and nurture the child whose parents, employed or not, are unable or unwilling to give the child the preschool education and values that are required in order for society to successfully begin his or her public school education.[14]

The child-care program, which would complement the tuition-certificate program, would have two major objectives. First, it would ensure that all children receive a head start, not merely to meet a minimum national standard but to enable each child to achieve his or her full potential. Second, it would ensure that all children are taught the basic values of society, providing the requisite foundation for commencing public education.

Here's how the child-care program would work. Every parent would receive a child-care certificate, similar to a tuition certificate, worth approximately $200 per month per child for children between the ages of eighteen months and five years. Like the tuition certificate, the child-care certificate could be redeemed by an approved provider of child-care services. Unlike the tuition certificate, the child-care certificate's redeemable value would be fixed; it would not vary based upon the performance of the service provider.[15]

Parents would be able to redeem the certificates for fixed-length sessions of child care, depending on the age of the child. For example, a child of eighteen to twenty-four months might be entitled to a three-hour session twice a week; at age 2, a three-hour session three times a week; at age 3, a three-hour session four times a week; and at age 4, a four-hour session five times a week.

Individual child-care sessions would concentrate on both preschool education and basic value instruction. Minimum standards would be developed for each, and parents would receive regular reports as to how

[14]The child-care programs could be incorporated into day-care programs (or vice versa). In this manner the dual function of child care for the children and day care for the parents could be simultaneously accomplished.

[15]The value of the certificates might eventually vary based upon performance, but would initially be fixed in order to facilitate implementation of the program.

their children were doing relative to both standards. Counselors would identify, and refer for special attention, children whose development fell behind what was expected of them.

Exactly how does one quantify a minimum social behavior standard for basic values? It's really not that difficult. Robert Fulghum, in his best-selling book *All I Really Need to Know I Learned in Kindergarten,* [16] may have already provided the simplistic but minimally requisite criteria. On his list:

> *Share everything.*
> *Play fair.*
> *Don't hit people.*
> *Put things back where you found them.*
> *Clean up your own mess.*
> *Don't take things that aren't yours.*
> *Say you're sorry when you hurt somebody.*

Our goal is to ensure that every child is entered in an approved child-care program. While it is likely that most parents would voluntarily (indeed, gladly) make use of their free child-care certificate, mandatory child care might be required—either for all, in the same manner that attendance in public school is now required, or in certain circumstances, such as where it was deemed necessary by a social worker or a court. Mandatory care could be implemented once child-care programs were widely available.

The prospect of 10 million or more children, each with a $200-per-month child-care certificate, would spawn preschool day-care and child-care industries of enormous proportions. And as with the privatization of education, these new industries would develop innovative methods for educating children and instilling social values that we cannot even begin to think of today. Day-care and child-care centers would become integral parts of virtually every apartment complex and neighborhood, as competitive providers emerged to offer these services at convenient locations for every child in America.

The costs of such a system are far outweighed by the gains to be

[16]Robert Fulghum, *All I Really Need to Know I Learned in Kindergarten* (New York: Villard Books, 1988), 6–7.

IMMIGRATION

> Give me your tired, your poor,
> Your huddled masses yearning to breathe free,
> The wretched refuse of your teeming shore,
> Send these, the homeless, tempest-tost, to me:
> I lift my lamp beside the golden door.[1]
> —Inscription on the base of the Statue of Liberty

IN THE United States today it is estimated that we have between 4 and 6 million criminals living and working among us. But unlike criminals who have committed a heinous act, the act of which these criminals are guilty has been committed by every one of us, or our parents, or their parents. Only when we or our forebears did it, it wasn't a crime.

These criminals are our illegal aliens, and the act that they committed was to risk everything they had, including their freedom and that of their families, in search of a better life in the United States. Like the immigrants who preceded them in the early 1900s, these individuals haven't come here demanding a better life; they have come for the opportunity to earn it. And although they make significant contributions to our national economy, they are being exploited by politicians seeking to capitalize on the xenophobic fears of uneducated Americans.

In the traditional economic world, with its fixed supply of resources,

[1]Lazarus, Emma, "The New Colossus," 1883.

one person's gain was another person's loss. The more people in a society, the more who had to share the finite economic pie. No wonder the initial reaction to immigration has been, "Why should I share what I have with someone else?" Even those in favor of open immigration often adopt this zero-sum view that we cannot afford to share what (little) we have with others. But, in today's alchemic economy, nothing could be further from the truth, for the immigrants are continually making *us* richer, not the other way around.

The Alchemist recognizes that virtually every person working in today's economy is a net economic plus to our nation. As we saw in Chapter 3, less than 5 percent of our gross national product—approximately $1,000 per person—produces enough food and shelter to keep every American alive. Each of us consumes approximately $1,000 per year in resources for minimal physical survival; most of our expenditures above this amount are for nonnecessities. This means that a family living in the United States with earnings in excess of $1,000 per member is contributing that excess to the wealth of our country. For example, a family of four earning only $10,000 a year is contributing approximately $6,000 annually to the national economy.

This has not always been so. There have been periods—for example, during the Great Depression—when the average American's cost of basic food and shelter exceeded the free-market value of his or her labor. At such times we may have been better off with fewer people in America. Each additional immigrant may have contributed a net economic loss to the national economy, because the cost of his or her basic needs exceeded the amount that person's labor contributed to the gross national product. It is interesting to note that the free market seems to know better than government policy when immigration is unprofitable, as evidenced by the fact that the number of people leaving the United States exceeded the number entering during each year from 1932 to 1936.[2]

But that was more than half a century ago, and it is highly unlikely that we will return to such a point at any time in the near future. As we saw in Chapter 3, the Great Depression was maintained by a lack of demand for goods and services. People were shocked by the speed

[2]Daniel B. Levine, Kenneth Hill, and Robert Warren, eds., *Immigration Statistics, A Story of Neglect* (Washington: National Academy Press, 1985), 15.

with which the Depression came upon them, and by the lack (relative to today) of available products above basic necessities; as a result, they refused to spend money for more than their essential needs. Today, and for the foreseeable future, nothing seems more unlikely. Today virtually the only thing everyone can agree on about consumer demand is that it is insatiable. Therefore, it is highly unlikely that there will soon come a time when every additional working person, legal or illegal, does not contribute positively to the national economy.

Our situation today is the same as it was during the tribal times of the hunter-gatherers: every additional worker adds significantly to the national wealth. Now that we understand this fact, let's alchemically analyze the issue of illegal immigration, starting with the history of legal immigration, to see what can be done for present U.S. citizens and for our brethren who wish to join us.

As suggested by the lines from Emma Lazarus' poem on the base of the Statue of Liberty, most of us have been brought up to think of America as the land of refuge for indigent and persecuted immigrants, the country that so generously offers refuge to all the world's oppressed people, no matter what the cost. Yet an accurate account of the immigration that built the United States into the most powerful nation on earth reveals a very different story. In fact, it is our erroneous collective recollection of the immigrant as the beneficiary of America, rather than of America as the beneficiary of the immigrant, that has led to the misguided immigration policy we have today.

From prerevolutionary times until the end of mass legal immigration in 1924, the United States was more the land of economic opportunity than of political freedom. Although most of us think of immigrants as free-thinking men and women who set sail to America for idealistic purposes, the truth is that the overwhelming majority of our ancestors came here for a simple economic reason—a better job.

In fact, encouraged by a progressive federal government that recognized the enormous benefits they could provide, many if not most immigrants were recruited in Europe and Asia by enterprising entrepreneurs and state governments.

The first federal policy to encourage immigration was proposed by no less a visionary than President Abraham Lincoln, in his annual message to Congress in 1863. Although Lincoln suggested that the

134

government actually pay the immigrants' passage, the final Act to Encourage Immigration, which was signed into law on July 4, 1864, merely allowed private employers to recruit foreign workers. The private companies were permitted to pay an immigrant's transportation expenses to the United States in return for a legally binding pledge of the worker's wages (as repayment for the cost of his or her passage) for up to twelve months.

Under this new law, which became known as the Contract Labor Act, private recruiters such as the American Emigrant Company were paid fees by both the employers for whom they contracted workers and the steamship lines that transported them. Early opposition to this program came not from xenophobic Americans, but from European interests that recognized the potential losses to their own industries. Thus in Europe, the American Emigrant Company often utilized U.S. consuls in order to carry out its work quietly and discreetly.[3]

In England, the press disparaged the U.S. recruiters, with one manufacturer protesting in 1865 that "the emigration of one spinner involves the stoppage of probably ten additional hands."[4] In France the same year, the government denied the U.S. consul at Marseilles permission to circulate copies of the Act to Encourage Immigration. And in Germany, the press was almost unanimously against emigration to America, accusing the U.S. government of "swindling" in passing the Act to Encourage Immigration.[5]

Meanwhile, in the United States, in addition to organized recruiting of immigrants by private employers, virtually every state and territory sought to recruit immigrants to their area. "At least 33 states and territorial governments eventually set up immigration bureaus, advertised in European and American foreign language newspapers, sent agents to northern and western Europe, and published their brochures, guidebooks, and maps in English, Welsh, German, Dutch, French, Norwegian, and Swedish,"[6] as well as Italian, and numerous Slavic and

[3]Charlotte Erickson, *American Industry and the European Immigrant: 1860–1885* (Cambridge: Harvard University Press, 1957), 25.

[4]Erickson, *American Industry,* 21.

[5]Erickson, *American Industry,* 25.

[6]Leonard Dinnerstein and David Reimers, *Ethnic Americans: A History of Immigration and Assimilation* (New York: New York University Press, 1977), 18.

Oriental languages. These states and territories recognized that immigrants were the key to turning American dreams into American accomplishments. In 1870, they even lobbied the federal government to assist their recruiting efforts when delegates from twenty-two states met in Indianapolis to petition Congress to establish a national immigration bureau.

The railroads worked as hard as the states to attract immigrants. Like the states, "the railroads subsidized agents in Europe, advertised and printed brochures in many languages, and played up the virtues of their respective territories. In addition, some gave free or reduced passage to prospective settlers, established immigrant receiving houses near their terminals, and built churches and schools for fledging communities."[7]

Thus, despite our collective nostalgic memory of our ancestors as "huddled masses yearning to breathe free," the reality is that the development of immigrant America is the story of a coordinated, public-private partnership consisting of our federal government, individual state governments, large corporations, and, most important, private entrepreneurs, formed for the purpose of furthering the economic development of our country.

While the original emphasis of most immigrant recruitment programs was on skilled labor, the majority of people recruited in this manner were unskilled workers who, interestingly, often were more productive than their skilled counterparts. As each industry advanced with the technological changes that were to make America the most powerful nation on earth, managers discovered that unskilled workers were the fastest to learn the new techniques. For example, in the steel industry, at every step of production involving technological change after 1880, managers discovered that it was easier to teach new methods to completely unskilled workers than to retrain skilled workers from related crafts and industries.[8]

Not all of the new immigrant workers, whether skilled or unskilled, adapted to America. Although the history books have recorded our immigration story as a one-way trip, the fact is that millions of the

[7]Dinnerstein and Reimers, *Ethnic Americans*, 19.

[8]James Howard Bridge, *The Inside History of the Carnegie Steel Company* (New York: Arno Press, 1972), 81. Originally published in 1903 as *The History of the Carnegie Steel Company*.

newcomers did *not* adapt to American life and willingly returned to their native countries. Between 1908 and 1914, immigration officials recorded 6,709,357 arrivals and 2,063,767 departures.[9] Looking back, it seems as though a process of "natural selection" occurred: the most adaptable immigrants found jobs and established families, while those who could not adapt returned home.

There was a major technological breakthrough in the 1850s that facilitated the trip for those wishing to emigrate and made it easier for those who couldn't adapt to return home. This breakthrough was the development of the steamship, which quickly replaced the sailing vessel originally used for transatlantic crossings. The steamship greatly shortened the trip from three months to ten days; by being able to travel inland European waterways, it made immigration possible from virtually the entire continent. According to the annual reports of the New York Commissioners of Immigration, as late as 1856, 96.4 percent of the immigrants arriving in New York came in sailing vessels; by 1873 an even higher percentage traveled in steamships.[10]

The United States was at the beginning of the alchemic age, an age where, as explained in Chapter 5, jobs would be eliminated by technological advances but society as a whole would be just as rich, because it would still receive the output of the displaced workers' jobs (now performed by machine). And, more important, society (and usually the displaced workers as well) would be even richer when the displaced workers found new, more productive jobs that added to the gross national product. However, although this alchemic process, which was soon to make the United States the wealthiest and most powerful nation in the history of the world, had begun, no one realized it at the time.

For example, the increased demand for shoes and boots spurred on by the Civil War accelerated the introduction of the McKay sewing machine, which greatly reduced the number of skilled bootmakers needed to produce a given number of boots. Although the reduced price for boots stimulated an increase in demand that increased the total number of bootmakers, it didn't matter to the individual boot-

[9]Dinnerstein and Reimers, *Ethnic Americans*, 39.

[10]Maldwyn Allen Jones, *American Immigration* (Chicago: The University of Chicago Press, 1960), 184.

maker who lost his job because the new bootmaking method didn't pay as much as his former position. Skilled workers were increasingly being replaced by new mechanical processes, and the new mechanical processes were increasingly operated by immigrants.

Mechanization was seen by the public as something that would cost them their jobs, not something that would get them more productive ones, and was viewed as the direct result of immigration. Less skilled or unskilled immigrants were considered incapable of learning skilled trades, and mechanization was seen as the response of manufacturers desirous of utilizing this cheaper labor, rather than as an independent, positive phenomenon that was developing on its own. To the skilled laborer or trade union member, mechanization and immigration went hand in hand and were to be resisted at all costs.

In hindsight, many skilled workers fared much better as a result of mechanization and immigration, either by becoming supervisors or by using their knowledge to become America's earliest entrepreneurs. But this was not a consideration to the workers fearing displacement, who never thought they would find *any* new job, let alone a better one.

Today, as we auspiciously look forward to new technological methods as the key to better and better lives, it is hard for us to appreciate the fear the nineteenth-century skilled worker had of mechanization. Back then, having a skill was more than the ability to earn a living—it was a way of life. In addition to current income, it provided social status through trade union membership and, most important, a legacy to pass on to one's children. Many family names (for example, Smith, Miller, and Brewer) were derived from such skilled professions.

Thus the immigrant, considered the cause of mechanization, was seen as the bane of the skilled worker. It didn't matter that often the skilled workers or trade union members were themselves immigrants; they saw themselves as "citizen workers" and viewed the newcomers, even those from their own former country, as somehow "different" and not entitled to share in the American dream. For example, Samuel Gompers, the influential president of the American Federation of Labor, who was himself a Jewish immigrant, saw no contradiction between his own origins and his advocacy for restrictions on new immigration.

Thus as the United States approached the twentieth century, the only thing growing faster than the numbers of new immigrants was the cumulative number of immigrants already here who saw themselves as "citizen workers," deserving of government protection from the newcomers. Although the country was on the rise through mechanization spurred on by immigration,[11] individual laborers and many government leaders didn't see the benefit of either and banded together to stop both.

When their efforts to halt immigration and mechanization failed, skilled labor tried to stop arriving immigrants from learning new techniques. For example, after the Civil War, when the McKay sewing machine was introduced to the boot- and shoe-making industry, a new trade union, the Knights of St. Crispin, was organized. The quest of these knights was to try to control the training of "greenhands" in order to safeguard the wages and employment of skilled boot and shoe workers.[12]

When labor leaders were unable to stop the new immigrants from learning new techniques, they took their case straight to the consumer. The union label was introduced for the first time in San Francisco in 1872 by white, unionized cigar makers to signal to consumers that their products were not manufactured by Chinese workers. The label was "white in color to indicate to the purchaser that he was buying a product manufactured by Caucasian workers."[13]

Each newly arriving group was seen as the scapegoat for the problems of those already here who were unable or unwilling to make their own American dreams come true, and the tactics taken against them included overt racism. Italians, the largest group of immigrants, were referred to as the "Chinese of Europe," and were said to be "just as bad as the Negroes." In the South, some Italians were forced to attend all-black schools, and in 1875 the *New York Times* said that it was "perhaps hopeless to think of civilizing them."[14] In a New Jersey mill town, several days of rioting erupted after a local firm hired fourteen

[11]In the steel industry from 1873 to 1908, the Bessemer converter and the open-hearth furnace made steel the first large-scale American industry, while the number of skilled puddlers in the entire country declined from 3,331 to about 2,000. Data from Erickson, *American Industry,* 127.

[12]Erickson, *American Industry,* 126.

[13]Vernon M. Briggs, Jr., *Immigration Policy and the American Labor Force* (Baltimore: Johns Hopkins University Press, 1984), 26.

[14]Dinnerstein and Reimers, *Ethnic Americans,* 40.

Jews, and, throughout America, job advertisements specified "Christians Only" or "No Jews Allowed."[15]

But no group, organized or disorganized, did more harm to the immigrants, and ultimately to America itself, than the Dillingham Commission, which was chartered by Congress in 1907 to report on the question of the new immigrants and the resultant mechanization of U.S. industry.

The commission, chaired by Senator William Dillingham from Vermont, blamed the new immigrants for depressing wages, causing unemployment, and hampering the development of trade unionism in America. The commission's biased report against mechanization and immigration created a "Dictionary of Races," in which were compiled ethnic and racial attributes to suggest that "the new immigrants (mostly southern and eastern European) were racially inferior to immigrants from western and northern Europe."[16]

The fifty-two–volume report of the commission took more than three hundred staff members over three years to complete and became the basis for a series of legislation that severely restricted the immigration of certain races, mainly those residing in southern and eastern Europe. Immigration from Asia and Africa was basically prohibited.[17]

The series of anti-immigration legislation culminated in the Immigration Act of 1924, which lowered the then-annual immigrant quota from 358,000 to 164,000, specifying that no more than 2 percent of the foreign-born population of each nationality of the Eastern Hemisphere residing in the United States in 1890 could be admitted in a given year. This meant, for example, that the quota for Italy declined from 42,000 to 4,000 persons; for Poland, from 31,000 to 6,000; and for Greece, from 3,000 to 100.[18] The 1924 act was also known as the Japanese Exclusion Act, because it banned immigration entirely for persons of Japanese ancestry, who had separately been declared ineligible for citizenship through naturalization by the U.S. Supreme Court in 1922. (The day the Immigration Act of 1924 took effect was de-

---

[15]Dinnerstein and Reimers, *Ethnic Americans*, 42.

[16]Dinnerstein and Reimers, *Ethnic Americans*, 37.

[17]The 1921 immigration act, which was originally vetoed by outgoing President Wilson but signed by President Harding, restricted immigration from Africa and Asia combined to about 3,000 immigrants per year. See Briggs, *Immigration Policy*, 43.

[18]Briggs, *Immigration Policy*, 45.

clared a national day of mourning in Japan.)[19]

Thus by 1924, the alchemic system of selective immigration based upon one's potential economic contribution came to an end. Legal immigration declined from over 1 million per year at the turn of the century to less than 50,000 per year during the restrictive 1930s. It has since risen to the approximately 500,000 to 600,000 per year allowed today, but since 1924 virtually all immigration has been based on racial or familial quotas, rather than on a free-market system based primarily on employment.

From a standpoint of what was best for the United States, our best and brightest Alchemists today couldn't have devised an immigration policy better than the one that existed prior to 1924. First, the open-market nature of the system encouraged only those who were willing to work to come and, once here, encouraged only those who were successful to stay. Second, federal legislation such as the Contract Labor Act ensured passage to America for anyone who wanted to work, provided a private-sector employer (who was allowed to freely recruit the best employees) was prepared to train and employ the person once he or she arrived. And third, state and local governments and large private employers competed with each other for the best immigrants, competitively distributing them throughout the land wherever their skills were needed.

In 1776, Adam Smith, in *The Wealth of Nations,* discussed how every individual, in the selfish pursuit of his own interests, is led by an "invisible hand" that ends up achieving the best good for all. Looking back on immigration prior to 1924, it's hard not to see that a *real* invisible hand was at work, recruiting the most highly motivated immigrants from every society in the world and guiding them to the state and the job where America needed them most.

The ancient alchemists believed that achievement of their magnum opus—the Great Work, or the ability to transmute less valuable base metals into very valuable gold—required, first and foremost, the right mental attitude. And although they never discovered how to make gold, in a sense they were successful in their quest, because their discoveries laid the foundation for modern science and modern medi-

---

[19]The Japanese exclusion provisions were not repealed until 1952. See Briggs, *Immigration Policy,* 45.

cine. That is, they passed on to their children the benefits that they expected to derive from the discovery of how to make gold—namely the ability to create great value where none existed before.

In many ways, the immigrants were much like the ancient alchemists. They faithfully believed that, regardless of their station in life, they could make themselves more valuable when they came to America. It was the strength of this faith in themselves and in their new country, more than anything else, that accounted for their success. And whether or not they achieved their goals in their own lifetime, by building the industrial and educational institutions that made America the greatest nation on earth, they passed on to their successors the benefits that they hoped to obtain for themselves in the New World.

The most important criterion for success as an immigrant today is the same as it was prior to 1924: faith in the American dream. It's the faith to believe that, regardless of a person's current station in life, the future can be influenced and improved, just as Galileo and Aristotle believed that it was within our power to understand how the world works and, by doing so, become master of our own destiny.

Today's system of legal immigration is a far cry from the original system that built this country. When immigration was open to virtually everyone, the individuals who came and stayed were primarily the ones who were able to obtain jobs, and the individuals who obtained jobs were the ones who contributed the most to the economy. By contrast, today the immigrant who can legally come to America is not necessarily the one who can add the most to our economy.

Our present system of legal immigration, which was established under the Immigration Reform Act of 1965, is based primarily on one's relationship to a U.S. citizen or legal permanent resident. Immigrants are admitted under two separate categories. Admission under the first category, which is limited to 270,000 persons annually, is based on a six-part preference system heavily weighted toward the applicant's relationship with an existing U.S. citizen or legal permanent resident. In 1987, 271,135 immigrants were admitted under this category.[20]

[20]Immigrants admitted under this category (271,135 in 1987) are determined under a point system of six preferences of which the first, second, fourth, and fifth are based on the alien's relationship with a U.S. citizen or legal permanent resident (217,262 in 1987) and the third and sixth are based on needed job skills (53,873 in 1987). See U.S. Department of Commerce, Bureau of the Census, *Statistical Abstract of the United States 1989* (Washington: Government Printing Office, 1989), 3, 11.

Admission under the second category, which is not subject to an annual limitation, includes immediate relatives of U.S. citizens, refugees, and other classes of special immigrants. In 1987, 330,381 immigrants were admitted under this category. Thus, the total legal immigration to the United States in 1987 was 601,516 persons.[21]

This discriminatory (but legal) system of immigration selects future U.S. citizens primarily on the basis of ancestry, rather than attitude or ability. Fortunately, however, we have another system of immigration, although an illegal one, that attracts individuals who can potentially make greater contributions to our country.

It is estimated that several million aliens illegally enter the United States each year, of which between 500,000 and 750,000 remain as illegal immigrants (the rest return to their home countries). Although estimates vary widely, most experts agree that the total illegal immigrant population in the United States today is between 4 and 6 million, approximately two-thirds of whom are of Mexican origin.

Unlike the approximately 600,000 legal immigrants admitted each year primarily to join their families, and just like our ancestors who came to the United States prior to 1924, virtually all of these illegal immigrants come to the United States for the same reason—a better job. Those who find a job remain, and those who don't return, since very few of them ever become recipients of public assistance.[22]

Study after study has shown that these illegal immigrants make positive contributions to the economy of the United States. In *The Gatekeepers—Comparative Immigration Policy*, a comprehensive book on U.S. immigration policy, Michael C. Lemay summarized the economic value of illegal immigrants when he wrote: "Virtually all of the experts agree that illegal immigration is a boon for employers and consumers."[23] And, in addition to the obvious economic benefits, the *Wall Street Journal* has continually observed that the U.S. government

---

[21]*Statistical Abstract of the United States 1989*, 3, 11.

[22]A study in San Diego County revealed only 10 undocumented immigrants in a review of 9,132 welfare recipient cases. And a similar review of 14,000 welfare recipient cases in Los Angeles County revealed only 56 undocumented aliens of which 54 were determined to have been eligible under current regulations.

See Jorge A. Bustamante, *The Immigrant Worker: A Social Problem or a Human Resource?* (Los Angeles: Institute of Industrial Relations, 1977), 15.

[23]Michael C. Lemay, *The Gatekeepers—Comparative Immigration Policy* (New York: Praeger Publishers, 1989), 10.

is receiving more from undocumented immigrants in the form of tax and social security deductions alone than the immigrants receive in public services.[24]

The principal economic arguments made against illegal immigrants—that they take jobs from U.S. citizens and drive down wages—are without merit. Some labor groups claim that illegal and legal immigrants take jobs away from minority citizens. But, according to the prestigious Hudson Institute, which conducts some of the best research in the labor field, "one statistical analysis of 247 metropolitan areas concluded that black unemployment rates are not increased by a rise in the proportion of Mexican immigrants in a local labor market. These results suggest that, to some extent, immigrants are complementary to, rather than in competition with, native minority workers."[25]

Most of the jobs in this country held by illegal immigrants are positions that Americans are not willing to take at any reasonable salary. As the economist John Kenneth Galbraith has argued, such jobs are usually filled by these immigrants at an "economical wage"—that is, a wage low enough to allow employers to make a profit, which enables them to remain in business. Reducing illegal immigration will not necessarily lead to a rise in wages and the employment of additional citizens. "When an employer is faced with the loss of cheap labor, there are other options besides raising wages to be considered: replacing workers with machines, moving the operation overseas, or simply going out of business. When the Bracero program (which allowed Mexicans to enter the United States to work for a limited period each year) ended in California, only the lettuce and citrus growers raised their wages in an attempt to attract domestic workers. The tomato growers began using mechanical harvesters, the asparagus growers moved to Mexico, and marginal growers in all crops simply closed down and sold their farms."[26]

The U.S. government, implicitly and often explicitly, has long recognized the tremendous benefit that working immigrants, even illegal immigrants, add to our economy. First, although politically the govern-

[24]"The Illegal Alien Non-Problem," *Wall Street Journal*, 18 June 1976, 8.

[25]*Workforce 2000—Work and Workers for the Twenty-first Century* (Indianapolis: Hudson Institute, 1987), 94.

[26]Lemay, *The Gatekeepers*, 10.

ment has generally denounced illegal immigration, the agency responsible for stopping it, the Immigration and Naturalization Service (INS), has never been adequately funded to effectively police our borders. Second, in recognition of the fact that illegal aliens pay hundreds of millions of dollars in federal income taxes (through employer withholding of part of their wages) but do not receive tax refunds or benefits, the Internal Revenue Service (IRS) does not generally share data on taxes it receives from illegal aliens with the INS, which is supposedly interested in apprehending illegal aliens, employed as well as unemployed. Third, and most important, the definition in the immigration law that makes it illegal to conceal, harbor, or shield an illegal alien contains an exception for employing them.[27] Thus, while it may be a crime for an illegal alien to work for a U.S. citizen, it traditionally was not been a crime for a U.S. citizen to employ an illegal alien.

This official tolerance changed when Congress passed the Immigration Reform and Control Act of 1986, which made it illegal for a U.S. citizen to employ an illegal alien. Suddenly, employers, even those citizens employing a domestic servant, were subject to a civil penalty of $250 to $10,000 for each illegal alien hired; and, for a "pattern or practice" of violations, an employer was subject to a $3,000 fine and six months' imprisonment. In order to improve enforcement, the act increased the INS budget from $593.8 million to over $1 billion.

While the 1986 act contains some positive provisions, such as a special amnesty program for certain categories of illegal immigrants, overall it is truly destructive to the long-term economic interests of both U.S. citizens and illegal immigrants.[28] First, by threatening jobs that America needs filled the act could damage important economic interests in the United States, particularly in the agricultural sector and in certain cities and towns in the Southwest. Second, by threatening

---

[27]The exception reads: "Provided, however, that for the purposes of this section, employment, including the usual and normal practices incident to employment, shall not be deemed to constitute harboring." (8 U.S.C., section 1324).

[28]The act offered legal temporary resident status (which would eventually lead to permanent resident status and potentially citizenship) to aliens who had entered the United States illegally before January 1, 1982, and to aliens who worked in U.S. agriculture for at least 90 days between May 1, 1985 and May 1, 1986. As of October 1, 1988, 1,764,600 aliens had applied under the first category and 890,300 under the second category. See *Statistical Abstract of the United States 1989*, 175.

rural communities are finding themselves without the tax base sufficient to support even basic services, such as hospitals and fire protection, let alone have the potential to attract new employers.) These depopulating areas have been unsuccessful in attracting citizens to relocate and many of them might even recruit new foreign immigrants if, as in the past, they were legally allowed to do so.

What is wrong with illegal immigration is contained in the word *illegal,* not *immigration.* Most of the problems of illegal immigrants will disappear when we begin treating these hard-working individuals in the manner they deserve to be treated, and stop forcing them to live as fugitives, subject to constant exploitation and crime. We can do this simply by giving them the opportunity to earn the citizenship that they so desperately seek.

However, in providing immigrants this opportunity, we cannot return to the totally open immigration policy of our past, because such a policy would not work today. In the nineteenth and early twentieth centuries, information and people traveled slowly. The 49 million people who came to the United States during that time did so over a span of approximately one hundred years, which allowed us time to receive, employ, and integrate them into our society on an orderly basis. Today, information and people travel quickly. Word of a totally open immigration policy would spread instantly worldwide, and people would begin arriving within days. Were we to reinstitute such a policy today, we might well receive 49 million immigrants during the first year we opened our borders.

Nor should we change the current dual-category system that admits approximately 600,000 relatives of existing citizens (and legal permanent residents) each year. True, those accepted under this system may not be the most economically productive persons available. However, as relatives of citizens, they are probably the people whose admission most enhances the lives of existing Americans. It would be wrong to abandon this policy which fosters family reunification, and we should not do so, because it highlights one of the many wonderful things that makes being a U.S. citizen so worthwhile.

What we should do is to establish, in addition to the current dual-category system, a new supplemental immigration system that will admit up to 3 million additional immigrants per year, approximately 1.2 percent per year of our total population, based primarily on one's potential contribution to the country. (From 1880 to 1920, U.S. immigration averaged 7.8 percent per year of the total U.S. population.)[34] This new supplemental immigration system should incorporate the following best elements of our past immigration policies.

First, it should encourage only those who are willing to work to come, and, once here, only those who are successful to stay. Second, anyone desirous of coming to the United States should be allowed to immigrate, provided a private-sector employer (who may freely recruit the best employees) is prepared to train and employ the person once he or she arrives. And third, state and local governments and private employers should be allowed to compete with each other for the best and brightest immigrants, competitively distributing them throughout the land wherever their skills are needed, thereby maximizing their contribution to our economy and ensuring a continuing array of job opportunities necessary to prevent their exploitation.

Here's how such a supplemental immigration system could be implemented. The federal government would pass enabling legislation allowing individual states, and private employers acting in concert with them, to recruit immigrants as legal working residents of the United States. After five years of employment, these immigrants could apply for permanent-resident status and citizenship under our present laws of naturalization. Such legislation would enable states (and their local municipalities) desirous of attracting immigrants to do so—provided, as explained later, that these entities were willing and able to provide assurances that the immigrants would make a positive contribution to the economy.

The enabling federal legislation would require that any state program established under it meet certain minimum standards. Foremost among them would be the requirements that any legal working resident brought in would: (1) have a job; (2) contribute to the economy an amount at least equivalent to the municipal services that he or she would use; (3) not adversely affect the employment opportunities of existing citizens; and (4) have a private or public entity guarantee that the alien would not become a public burden if the job terminated.

Specifically, such a program for a given state might work as follows. A private employer would contract with the state to establish a manu-

---

[34]*Statistical Abstract of the United States 1989,* 9.

facturing plant employing, say, 5,000 persons in a city or town that would benefit from an increase in population. The employer would be responsible for recruiting and training the immigrant employees. In addition to recruiting abroad, illegal aliens, unemployed citizens, and other U.S. residents would be encouraged to apply (some states might even pass incentives for employing certain disadvantaged groups). Special withholding taxes of part of the immigrants wages', in some cases matched by the private employers, would ensure that the local municipality would not be burdened by the social services used by the recruited employees.

An immigrant in this supplemental immigration program would receive a five-year work permit entitling him or her to work at any job that was registered with the federal government to employ such legal working residents. The employee would thus be able to change jobs, which would help ensure against exploitation of the immigrant by the employer. If the employee was terminated, he or she would have ninety days to find employment at another job registered in the program, even a job located in another state.

Individual states and their immigrant employers would have to ensure, perhaps by posting bonds, that unemployed legal working residents would not remain in the United States. Immigrants who lost their jobs would either be transported back to their country of origin or assisted in finding employment elsewhere in the program.

Certain states might designate whole geographic areas to be Free Immigration Zones (FIZ), in which any company could hire legal working residents. For example, an economically depressed area that was losing population might be designated a FIZ in hopes of attracting new immigrants and companies desirous of employing them. There are already many Free Economic Zones (FEZ) in the United States, where companies are allowed to manufacture and store goods without tariffs in hopes of generating increased economic activity. In our alchemic world, where labor is capital, the establishment of a Free Immigration Zone (FIZ) might prove more beneficial to the local economy than the ability to manufacture and store goods without tariffs.

Key to this supplemental immigration proposal is that each program set up under it would be different, each state would design the optimal program to meet the needs of its own citizens and municipalities. And despite how successful immigration to the United States has been in the past, it could be even more beneficial in the future if each state is ready to examine how immigration worked in its past and apply the lessons it has already learned. In addition, certain states with large populations of unskilled U.S. citizens might require employers to hire and train a certain number of unemployed citizens for each immigrant employed in the supplemental immigration program.

To take advantage of productive labor overseas, U.S. multinationals have constructed manufacturing plants around the world, *exporting* not just U.S. jobs but some of our best and brightest managers and technology. In today's alchemic economy, where products have shorter life-cycles and distribution is becoming more and more important, companies that manufacture products close to their customers have decided advantages. If the productive labor supply were available, multinationals would build more of their newest plants inside the United States, *importing* not just U.S. jobs, but some of the world's best and brightest managers and technology.

While in the past it may have made sense to build plants employing thousands in Brazil or Korea, in the future it may make more sense to build these plants inside the United States, importing thousands of productive Brazilians and Koreans who wish to work here and become U.S. citizens. If we can keep the wages paid from these jobs inside our country, even when paid to specifically imported foreign workers, the wages will be recirculated many times over in our economy as these new workers purchase their housing, food, and other necessities from U.S. suppliers.

The supplemental immigration program, along with the retraining of existing U.S. workers and the improvement of our public educational system, will ensure that the critical labor supply in our country is available to allow for more jobs to be established in the United States and for our continued economic growth.

The Theory of Alchemy teaches us how every additional productive person is a benefit to all of us, for each productive person adds to our overall level of technology, which controls and defines our level of physical resources. Thus we have the physical resources to support a virtually unlimited number of productive people, because it is the number of productive people that really determines our level of physical resources. And in the United States of America, where we have the living space along with the physical resources for potentially tens of millions of productive immigrants, we also have a critical need for productive people just to continue our existing economic life-style.

But in the United States, perhaps the only thing greater than our capacity to absorb more productive people is our desire to share the American dream with all of those who want to help us carry it into the twenty-first century.

HOW JAPAN ALMOST BECAME NUMBER ONE

If the question is whether Japan's system is archaic or whether America's system is an industrial castoff, I think we can say that Japan's system is at the leading edge.[1]

—Toshio Yamaguchi, former minister of labor, Japan[1]

THE TURN of the century marked the beginning of America's alchemic age, an age in which technological advances—which then meant the mechanization of production—began to yield an abundance of what was once thought to be scarce resources.

On a visit to the United States in the 1920s, Winston Churchill was impressed with our productivity, stating that:

> Never before had such immense quantities of goods of all kinds been produced, shared, and exchanged in any society. There is, in fact, no limit to the benefit which human beings may bestow upon one another by the highest exertion of their diligence and skill.[2]

[1]Bill Powell and Bradley Martin, "What Japan Thinks of Us," *Newsweek*, 2 April 1990, 21.

[2]James Gooch, Michael George, and Douglas Montgomery, *America Can Compete* (Dallas: The Institute of Business Technology, 1987), 21.

Yet only a few decades earlier, America was still an agrarian society compared to Great Britain, which dominated manufacturing and world trade. What happened in so short a time that the United States surpassed Great Britain, the country from which it had learned virtually all of its manufacturing techniques? What caused the student to pass the teacher? The answer is simple: America discovered technology gaps, and utilized new technology to better itself.

History has now repeated itself. A sequence of events, comparable to those that transformed the relationship between Great Britain and the United States, reversed the post-World War II relationship between the United States and Japan. The technology gaps that were discovered and implemented in the United States in the early 1900s, and in Japan in the 1960s, involved better ways of utilizing or *managing* technological resources in manufacturing—technology gaps in the process of implementing other technology gaps. As we shall see, advances in *managing* technological resources can be as impressive as advances in technological resources themselves.

At the close of the nineteenth century, most U.S. manufacturing industries were organized around the apprentice-craft system, in which the worker learned his own trade and supplied his own tools. Management's job was merely to divide the work among the workers and see that they did it, rather than provide guidance or training to improve their labors.

Frederick W. Taylor (1856–1914), an American inventor and engineer, felt that there was a tremendous waste of both labor and material in this manufacturing process. Taylor developed a new system, which he called scientific management, premised upon the belief that "Management is responsible for designing and developing the methods by which work is done; it must not be left up to the skill and initiative of the worker."[3] Under Taylor's theory, managers had to do more than merely hire the best workers they could find and order them to work; it was incumbent upon managers to develop job techniques and teach them, thereby enabling the workers to better perform their jobs.

Taylor once served as a consultant at a steel plant in Bethlehem, Pennsylvania. At the plant, about 600 laborers shoveled heavy iron ore, light ash, and other substances. Each substance differed in weight. A

[3]Gooch, George, and Montgomery, *America Can Compete*, 11–12.

shovelful of the ore weighed about thirty pounds; a shovelful of the ash weighed about four pounds. The workers supplied their own shovels, and they used the same shovel for each substance. Taylor, noticing that the employees tired quickly, conducted experiments in which he found that a twenty-one-pound load was the most comfortable. Accordingly, he designed shovels of various sizes—one for each substance—so that a shovelful of each substance, when lifted with the proper shovel, weighed twenty-one pounds. After Taylor distributed the redesigned tools and instructed the workers in their use, the work of 600 men was performed by 140. The number of tons moved per day per worker rose from sixteen to fifty-nine, wages increased 60 percent, and the cost of moving the material fell 50 percent, even with the increased wages.[4]

The relatively simple technology gap that Taylor discovered at the steel mill was a way of improving production through scientific management—that is, the development and implementation of a better way to do the work. Taylor's principle of scientific management was widely implemented throughout America with equally impressive results. For example, when applied to the 5,000-year-old method of bricklaying, the trade was divided into four separate functions and specific tools were designed for each. As a result, productivity increased from 120 to 350 bricks per man per day.[5] All of this innovation contributed to the increased productivity that led to Churchill's comment on American productivity in the 1920s.

This first major technology gap in the process of implementing other technology gaps—scientific management—was concerned with just the supply-side of the manufacturing equation: how to manufacture more goods that people want at a lower price. As a result of this supply-side breakthrough, the industrial revolution in the United States, in less than two decades, surpassed the industrial revolution in England, the country where it had originated. But as we shall see, this supply-side innovation was displaced by demand-side innovations in how to manufacture types of goods that people will want *more*, even

---

[4]Gooch, George, and Montgomery, *American Can Compete*, 12.

[5]This was accomplished by Frank Gilbreath, one of Taylor's contemporaries. He devised a system which set up the bricks and the bricklayer on a movable table, the height of which was raised as the wall went up, used a special mortar box and trowel, which required only a single scoop per brick, and adjusted the mortar consistency to eliminate the need for tapping the brick. See Gooch, George, and Montgomery, *America Can Compete*, 13.

at a higher price. And although these demand-side innovations originated in America in the 1920s, they were widely copied and improved
upon by the Japanese in the 1960s, who used them to surpass the U.S.
manufacturing industry in which they were born.

In 1909, the Ford Motor Company used scientific management to
revolutionize the U.S. automobile industry. Prior to then, cars were
symbols of class distinction and Ford—like most other carmakers—
made beautiful but expensive cars. (Indeed, this led Woodrow Wilson
to remark that "Nothing spreads socialism as automobiles.") But that
year Henry Ford embarked on his most ambitious project: to build a
popularly priced car. What made the project so ambitious was the fact
that there was no existing market for such an item.

Ford set out to build an affordable car by designing a practical
automobile and utilizing the best scientific management techniques
available to produce it—or as a modern-day Alchemist would say, by
finding and implementing technology gaps at every stage of the manufacturing process. And, in a classic example of alchemic demand creation, as Ford drove the price through the floor, there seemed to be
no ceiling on the number of people who wanted his cars. The table
here, taken from an excellent book which describes in more detail how
Ford did it, illustrates what happened:[6]

Year	Sales Price of Model T Runabout	Ford Motor Sales (millions)	Net Income (millions)
1908	$850	$ 4.7	$ 1.1
1909	$750	9.0	3.0
1910	$680	16.7	4.1
1911	$590	24.6	7.8
1912	$525	42.5	13.5
1913	$500	89.1	27.1
1914	$440	119.4	33.0
1915	$390	121.1	30.0
1916	$345	206.8	57.0

[6]Gooch, George, and Montgomery, *America Can Compete*, 18.

While Henry Ford obviously understood alchemic supply-side or quantity demand—technology's ability to expand existing demand through making goods available at a lower price—he failed to understand alchemic demand-side or quality demand—technology's ability to expand existing demand through making different and better goods available, even at a higher price. And as we shall see, it was this eventual consumer shift from quantity to quality demand—something, as illustrated in Chapter 3, the Japanese have understood better than anyone else—that nearly cost him his company.

From 1920 to 1921 sales of Ford automobiles soared from 690,755 to 933,720 units, and the company's profits rose from $53 million to $75 million. By contrast, during the same period Chevrolet sales fell from 134,117 to 58,080 units, and General Motors, whose overall sales dropped from $567 million to $304 million, reported a $38 million loss.

But GM didn't give up. Alfred Sloan, its chairman, reasoned that it would have been "suicidal" to try to compete with Ford in the low-price field, so he decided to go after the Ford owner who might want to trade in his Model T for a higher quality vehicle, even at a higher price.

Sloan added some operational features, such as an automatic starter, to his competitive Chevrolet "K" model, but mainly concentrated on using technology to enhance the appeal and individuality of the product. For example, he offered a wide choice of colors and instituted annual model changes to stimulate demand on a recurring basis. The strategy worked, as illustrated by the next table:[7]

| | CHEVROLET | | FORD | |
Year	Unit Volume	Unit Price	Unit Volume	Unit Price
1925	481,000	$735	1,652,000	$580
1926	692,000	695	1,379,000	565
1927	940,277	645	364,000	495

Henry Ford had adopted an alchemic supply-side strategy: he believed that he could sell anything so long as it was popularly priced. But Ford made two mistakes that an Alchemist would not make today.

[7]Gooch, George, and Montgomery, *America Can Compete*, 24.

First, he succeeded in building a highly efficient production system in part by allowing no variety in the product (he often remarked that he would sell you a car in "any color you want, so long as it's black"), but he failed to build in the ability to efficiently change *what* he was producing. Ford realized that technology could be used to create great value by lowering the price of physical goods—Supply-Side Alchemy—but he didn't foresee that the product he was making today would be obsolete in the marketplace tomorrow—Demand-Side Alchemy. His highly efficient production system, which General Motors never came close to matching in terms of cost per unit, got much of its efficiency by being inflexible; that is, it was only efficient in making large quantities of a single product.

Second, and more important, Ford failed to realize that in the alchemic world the market cannot be cornered, from either the supply or the demand side. No matter how strong the demand for a product, eventually someone will discover and implement a new technological gap in the manufacturing process that will undermine another person's "corner" on the market. And while Ford succeeded in his day on the supply side, his market was penetrable from the demand side, as Ford saw when General Motors offered something his customers wanted *even more than low price.*

What happened in the 1920s between Ford and General Motors is analogous to what happened in the last two decades between the United States and Japan. General Motors beat Ford by making a more desirable new product, rather than a less expensive version of the same product. It is ironic, therefore, that General Motors, as the largest U.S. automaker, has lost more to the Japanese automakers than any other automobile manufacturer in the United States—for the same reasons it succeeded at beating Ford fifty years earlier.

In 1945, the U.S. automobile industry was the envy of the world, mainly for its ability to mass-produce enormous quantities of similarly designed automobiles at reasonable prices. As the years went by, the industry made great strides in improving the technology of manufacturing a single product—Supply-Side Alchemy—but it neglected to make strides in improving the technology of the product itself—Demand-Side Alchemy. On the demand side, the industry emphasized price competition and cosmetic differences, putting less emphasis on discovering what the consumer might want in the product but wasn't getting—such as enhanced performance, state-of-the-art electronics, and better reliability and quality.

The automobile is a complex product, typically requiring the assembly of 15,000 or more parts per vehicle. And the use of these parts incorporates many different technologies (metallurgy, electronics, plastics, and so on), each of which is constantly evolving. The successful production of the most advanced automobiles requires an ability to best utilize these many different technologies.

Unfortunately, the U.S. automobile manufacturing industry in the postwar years was not designed to make the best use of rapidly advancing technologies. The production emphasis of U.S. automakers was on large-scale production runs of similar vehicles, in order to spread the cost of setting up the plant among millions of units. And, of course, large production runs required large inventories of finished parts to keep the assembly lines rolling. While this enabled manufacturers to produce the maximum quantity of a specific vehicle at the lowest price, it also made it extremely expensive to introduce new designs and technological innovations. Even the slightest change in the product could cost millions of dollars in retooling expenses, and many parts had to be scrapped when major new designs were introduced.

The system was also ineffective from a standpoint of product quality. Owing to the large inventories required to maintain continuous production, individual parts and subproducts were often produced in large numbers and stored until they were needed rather than put to immediate use. As a result, poor quality or poorly designed components were often not discovered until many defective parts had been either manufactured or already installed in thousands of vehicles.

During Japan's postwar reconstruction, the Japanese automakers, at the urging of their Ministry of International Trade and Industry (MITI), originally tried to copy the U.S. system of mass-production. But their domestic market at the time did not demand enough units of a single vehicle to justify tooling the large plant required to produce them. Moreover, on the supply side, there were many automakers, all backed by large conglomerates; no single company could be assured of capturing a large enough portion of the market to justify mass-production of a single car. And on the demand side, unlike the U.S. marketplace, which produced large quantities of one type of vehicle (the

159

family sedan), Japanese consumers demanded many different types of trucks and cars.[8]

As a result, Japanese automakers were forced to develop cost-effective methods for low-volume production runs. They did this in two ways. First, they developed flexible machinery that could be used to make more than one model or product. Second, since they couldn't afford to maintain the large inventories required for mass-production, they developed manufacturing processes that produced needed components simultaneously rather than sequentially, as in the U.S. system, thereby eliminating the need to store large inventories of parts. These smaller production runs and the techniques developed to accomplish them—flexible machinery and simultaneous parts manufacturing—were not designed to be as cost-efficient as the U.S. system. But they had two very important, if unintended, benefits that eventually enabled the Japanese automobile industry to surpass its U.S. counterpart.

First, with flexible machinery designed to produce different types of automobiles, it was far less expensive to retool as automobile technology advanced. Thus, technological advances such as electronic fuel injection, disc braking systems, and unitized body construction could be added as they were developed, and at relatively low cost. These advances in product design became especially important selling points when the pace of innovation accelerated during the 1970s.

Second, and more important, by developing a manufacturing system that was not dependent on large parts inventories, the Japanese stumbled onto something that was to make them the world's largest and most efficient automaker: improved quality.[9]

One of the greatest expenses in conventional manufacturing is the cost to repair or reject defective units. This is especially critical in the automobile industry, where it isn't feasible to reject a $10,000 automobile because of a defective $50 part, but where it can cost thousands

[8]Michael L. Dertouzos, Richard K. Lester, and Robert M. Solow, *Made in America—Regaining the Productive Edge* (Cambridge, Mass.: MIT Press, 1988), 180.

[9]Reuters reported on January 25, 1990, that the Japan Automobile Manufacturers said that Japanese automakers produced 13.03 million vehicles in 1989, up 2.6 percent from 1988. In 1989, 10.85 million vehicles were produced in the United States.

of dollars in labor and management time to find the defective part and replace it. In the U.S. automobile industry there is a significant time delay between the manufacture or purchase of component parts and their eventual use. Therefore, when a part is improperly made or poorly designed, the defect may not be noticed until after an entire production run has been completed, by which time the defective part may have been installed in every unit produced. The Japanese automobile industry, by contrast, which generally manufactures parts as they are needed and is therefore less reliant on large parts inventories, is less susceptible to a large production run of defective units. From a quality-control standpoint, the Japanese therefore had a major, albeit unintended, advantage over their U.S. counterparts. This actually made the Japanese system more cost-effective than the U.S. system, which it was *not* designed to beat.

This Japanese system of manufacturing, which developed because their society couldn't justify large production runs, is today called the Just-in-Time (JIT) system, owing to its reduction or elimination of inventories. And while various theories have been advanced to explain the Japanese manufacturing success (for example, the fact that they work in small teams and have a homogeneous labor supply), virtually all experts today agree that the JIT system is to be given most of the credit.

The JIT system, the synchronization of an organization's sales and production processes so that a component or finished product is produced "just in time" to meet its current demand, is one of the major technological advances of our Alchemic age. However, as many U.S. manufacturers discovered in the 1980s when they unsuccessfully tried to copy it, a JIT system takes so long to plan and implement that it is really beneficial only to those industries, such as automobile manufacturing and steel production, that are characterized by long lead times between product design and product manufacture, a great amount of product differentiation, and high customer loyalty.[10]

When some U.S. companies initially had difficulty implementing JIT systems, a few experts believed that the systems might work well only in Japan because of specific Japanese cultural characteristics or

[10]Ernest H. Hall, Jr., "Just-In-Time Management: A Critical Assessment," *Executive* (Summer 1989): 315–18.

bearings be lubricated at the plant in Japan before shipment, eliminating an entire manufacturing step for the Indiana firm. And, most important, the Japanese engineers arranged to visit the Indiana plant every six months in order to continually improve the plant's use of the product, further enhancing the relationship with their new customer.

Representatives of the Chicago supplier hadn't visited their Indiana customer's plant even once during the fifty years they had done business, yet the Japanese engineers made a point of traveling—all the way from Japan—twice a year to ensure the best use of their product. No wonder the Japanese are beating the U.S. manufacturers!

Hope for U.S. industry can be found in the epilogue to this story. The Indiana company soon began visiting its own customers on a regular basis, providing the same customer assistance that the Japanese had given them.

Since the beginning of their current golden age, the Japanese have understood that the customer, not the product, is the most important part of the alchemic manufacturing equation. Just as technology has made physical resources so plentiful that controlling them is no longer the key to riches, technology has also made the actual manufacturing of physical products so widespread that simply making them more efficiently is no longer the key to riches. The Japanese have found that the key to manufacturing riches in today's Alchemic world is making just what the customer wants—knowing what to make rather than just knowing how to make it. And the Japanese JIT production system— which starts with the product the customer wants at the time he or she wants it, and then works backwards to set up all the manufacturing schedules—is the best manufacturing system today, not just because of improved quality control or reduced inventories, but because of its virtual single-minded devotion to the needs of the customer.

The Japanese built an entire manufacturing empire based on consumer demand; they realized that the key to manufacturing riches is in making products that are *pulled* by, rather than *pushed* to, the customer.

The Japanese earned their success with their extraordinary commitment to the needs of customers. But this single-minded devotion to customer satisfaction, which accounted for the rise in Japanese industrial power, may be responsible for Japan's decline as well.

WHY JAPAN ISN'T GOING
TO MAKE IT

In Japan, however, self-destruction is exalted as it is nowhere else.[1]
—Robert Elegant, *Pacific Destiny*

By 1987, Japan had the world's highest gross national product—
$19,322 per person—slightly above the per capita GNP of the United
States, which was $18,413.[2] But figures like this mask the fact that the
Japanese economy is on the verge of a crisis. Although Japan is widely
believed to be one of the world's wealthiest nations, an alchemic analysis of its economic situation indicates otherwise.

An economist measures wealth by dividing a society's gross national
product by the number of people who share it. Measured this way, the
Japanese economy is quite healthy. An Alchemist, however, measures
the wealth of a society by examining how well the individuals really live
as compared to a statistical "reality" of their per capita GNP. And
under this quality-of-life analysis, Japan is far from rich. For example,
the per capita GNP of Malaysia, at $2,038, is only about 10 percent

[1]Robert Elegant, *Pacific Destiny: Inside Asia Today* (New York: Crown Publishers,
1990), 100.

[2]U.S. Department of Commerce, Bureau of the Census, *Statistical Abstract of the
United States 1989* (Washington: Government Printing Office, 1989), 823.

as high as that of Japan.[3] Yet by most measures of human comfort—housing space, clothing, food, and recreation—the two societies are about the same.[4]

In Japan, GNP has risen an impressive 177 percent over the past ten years.[5] But this growth has been surpassed by the cost of maintaining their life-styles for two reasons: (1) the Japanese internal economy is terribly inefficient, and (2) Japanese wealth is increasingly only paper wealth.

In manufacturing, Japan's reputation for efficiency is second to none. But in internal distribution, Japan is one of the most inefficient nations in the world. As we saw in Chapter 2, a product selling in the United States for $100 reflects about $20 in manufacturing costs (labor and materials) and about $80 in distribution costs (getting the product from the manufacturer to the retailer). In Japan, the same product can probably be made for even less than $20, but its distribution costs can run 50 percent to 100 percent higher than in the United States, owing primarily to an archaic distribution system fostered by Japanese politics.

In the 1920s, the United States had thousands of mom-and-pop retail stores. Despite our nostalgic recollections of homey shops with friendly service and a personal touch, from an economic standpoint these stores were terribly inefficient and charged exorbitant markups. As large chains like Sears and K-Mart took root in our suburbs and cities, most of these smaller stores were eliminated. The few survivors—which continued to charge their customers far too much while offering poorer service and less selection—have recently been replaced as entrepreneurs like Sam Walton found ways to put stores like Wal-Mart across small-town America. But the mom-and-pop stores didn't roll over without a fight. In the 1930s, as the operators of these inefficient shops saw an approaching end to their ability to reap high markups, they sought to bar chain stores entirely. When that failed, they tried using fair trade laws to prohibit the selling of brand-name merchandise below their own higher prices. Fortunately for the American

[3]*Statistical Abstract of the United States 1989*, 822.

[4]James Fallows, *More Like Us* (Boston: Houghton Mifflin Co., 1989), 42.

[5]Japanese GNP from 1977 to 1987 rose 177 percent. See *World Tables 1988–1989 Edition* (Baltimore: Johns Hopkins University Press, 1989), 16–17.

consumer, the courts held that it wasn't illegal for the new chain stores to market their goods at competitive prices, and today the United States has the most efficient retail system in the world, offering an endless variety of merchandise at prices that most Americans can afford.

In Japan, a similar battle looms between the mom-and-pop stores, which want to retain their monopoly on exorbitant markups, and discount retailers, both foreign and Japanese, who seek to serve this lucrative market by offering quality goods at competitive prices. But in Japan, the good guys are losing.

Retail stores larger than 500 square meters (5,382 square feet) cannot be built without permission from the Japanese government. Existing stores of this size require government permission to expand, extend their hours of operation, or change the days of the month they close. Proposed stores larger than 1,500 square meters must obtain the unanimous approval of smaller retailers in the area, something virtually impossible to do. The result of these restrictions is that 83 percent of Japan's 1.5 million retailers employ fewer than five people.[6]

However, the inefficiency of this archaic system of retailing pales in comparison to Japan's multilevel wholesale distribution system. In Japan, goods pass through as many as eight or more levels of distribution between the manufacturer and the retailer. At some of these levels, people never even physically touch the goods, but their positions are protected by government regulations. Approximately 18 percent of the Japanese work force is engaged in distribution, almost twice the U.S. percentage.[7] Although this artificially inflates prices, the vast number of workers employed provides a large enough political force to ensure the system's survival. Indeed, the fact that Japan can afford such publicly sanctioned featherbedding in its all-important distribution sector is a testament to the efficiency of the county's production capability.

One of the most absurd results of this inefficient distribution system

[6]Robert E. Weigand, "So You Think Our Retailing Laws Are Tough?" *Wall Street Journal*, 13 November 1989, A10.

[7]"To have and have not in Japan," *U.S. News and World Report*, 13 February 1989, 41. Approximately 10 percent of the U.S. labor force worked in retail distribution (excluding food service) in 1986. See U.S. Department of Labor, Bureau of Labor Statistics, *Projections 2000* (Washington: Government Printing Office, 1988), 41.

has been the importation of Japanese goods. Japanese retailers have actually bought Japanese-made goods in the United States, at prices far less than they cost in Japan, and imported them to Japan to sell there at lower-than-normal prices. In one instance, an imported Japanese cordless telephone, selling in Japan for one-eighth its regular Japanese price, was outselling the identical, nonimported item ten to one. The manufacturer, Matsushita Electric Trading Company, repurchased all of the imported models at the Japanese importer's full price just to get them off the market.[8]

The distribution of manufactured goods is not the only inefficient area of Japan's economy. Equally ineffective is the country's system of food production, which in turn has a deleterious effect on the housing market. In Japan, rice is grown on tiny plots that constitute half of the nonmountainous land in the country. Production is so inefficient that the Japanese consumer pays up to ten times the world's price for rice. But the plots are protected by prohibitions against the importation of rice and tax laws ensuring that the rice paddies remain as farmland rather than as more needed residential plots. On average, the Japanese (who overall eat considerably less food than Americans) spend about 30 percent of their income on food; American food expenses, by contrast, amount to only about 15 percent of a person's income.[9] And Japan's farm subsidy takes a greater toll on the Japanese consumer than just higher food prices; it has caused a critical shortage of housing that threatens the country's social structure as well as the economic life-style of its citizens.

A great deal of Japan's land is dedicated to farming, and government policy discourages the development of much of the rest. As a result, the price of both land and housing in postwar Japan has soared.[10] The average Japanese worker pays six times his or her annual salary to purchase a house half the size of the average U.S. home. Moreover, the

[8]James Fallows, *More Like Us* (Boston: Houghton Mifflin Co., 1989), 42.

[9]Author Robert Elegant tells of following "the progress of apples grown in Aomori, three hours by fast train from Tokyo, through the hands of more than a dozen middlemen to the final purchasers in Tokyo's Marunouchi district. Starting at twenty-five cents, each apple cost the consumer four dollars." See Elegant, *Pacific Destiny*, 146.

[10]In 1986 alone the cost of real estate in Tokyo rose 54 percent. "Is Japan as Rich as You Think?" *Newsweek*, 8 June 1987, 48.

infrastructure surrounding these homes is generally inadequate; for example, only 36 percent of Japanese homes have sewage service, compared to 74 percent for the United States and 80 to 90 percent for most developed nations.[11]

Moreover, the spiraling price of land in Japan is wreaking havoc with what had once been a remarkably even distribution of income. As recently as 1985, the landholdings of the richest fifth of Japan's population were only 5.5 times greater than those of the middle fifth. But by 1987, this disparity had nearly doubled.[12] More than half a million Tokyo families now count as *nyuu ritchi,* or "new rich," because they own properties that have soared to inflated values of $1 million or more.[13]

Although the United States has twenty-five times the acreage of Japan, the total value of Japan's real estate is four times greater than America's. A piece of land in Tokyo the size of your footprint is worth about $8,000. But overall, the land-price spiral has not created any real *nyuu ritchi.* Unlike Japan's alchemic manufacturing industry—which has created real value in something that was less valuable before—the land-price spiral is merely the result of a minority of Japanese citizens bidding up the price of land among themselves; there is no real creation of value for the overall society.

However, the most significant economic problem facing the Japanese today is not what they are doing with their newfound manufacturing riches; it's what they are *not* doing with it—spending it. The Japanese are notorious hoarders; and, as we shall see, this hoarding poses a very serious threat to their economy. In Chapter 3, we saw that the primary factor sustaining the Great Depression was a lack of demand for consumer goods. In the 1930s, the U.S. government and the private sector tried unsuccessfully to get consumers to trust the system again and resume spending, but nothing short of a major world war was

[11]*Statistical Abstract of the United States 1989,* 825.

[12]Urban C. Lehner, "Disparities in Wealth Affront Japan's Vision of Itself as Classless," *Wall Street Journal,* 20 June 1989, A1.

[13]A recent *U.S. News and World Report* article, entitled "To Have and Have Not in Japan," examined the potential for political unrest in Japan as the distribution of income, primarily because of the land-price spiral, widens. "To Have and Have Not in Japan," *U.S. News and World Report,* 13 February 1989, 41–42.

able to get the economy going. It is hoped that the Japanese will have an easier solution ahead of them as we now begin to examine this serious problem in their economy.

Let's return to the island described in Chapter 5, with its ten fishermen and their families. Initially, all of the men worked as fishermen, catching just enough fish to meet the island's needs. Then a new method of fishing was developed—the net—which allowed two men to catch as many fish as ten used to catch with their lines. As a result, two men could now supply all the fish the island's inhabitants could consume.

Of course, the island had to deal with eight unemployed fishermen. But suppose that another land (the mainland) agreed to purchase from the island four times the amount of fish that the islanders could consume, which (coincidentally for our example) is exactly the amount that the eight unemployed fishermen could catch. Now all ten fishermen were employed again, catching five times as many fish as they used to catch with their lines. The mainland paid the islanders with its own paper currency, which the islanders could use to purchase anything the mainland produced. The fishermen on the island fished and fished for many years, accumulating lots of the mainland's paper currency.

As the years went by, however, the people of the mainland noticed that the islanders weren't purchasing many of the mainland's products with the paper currency that they were accumulating. At first this was because the islanders were cautious with their new wealth and hoarded it. But when they had accumulated enough currency that they began to consider spending it, they hadn't developed an appetite for most of the things that the mainland had for sale. (Looked at another way, since the islanders hadn't been buying any of the mainland's goods, the mainland's manufacturers hadn't gone out of their way to make any goods that the islanders might want.) Moreover, the elders of the island, fearful of becoming dependent on imports, passed laws heavily taxing the fishermen's earnings and prohibiting the importation of the few mainland goods that the islanders wanted.

Over time, the island accumulated so much of the mainland's currency that the elders began lending it to the mainland's government and individuals. In addition, the islanders began purchasing mainland real estate, believing that this was a good investment. Every day, the islanders were told by their elders how rich they were, but actually life on the island hadn't changed much since they started fishing with the nets. The only real difference was that now they worked much longer hours and paid huge taxes to their government, which lent the money to the mainland.

Meanwhile, on the mainland life was grand. The mainland people stopped working as much because of all the fish they got from the island. They started spending much more time with their families; developed interests in the arts and new recreational activities; and, with the money they borrowed from the island, they built new roads, sewage systems, and military facilities. As time went on, it seemed as if the mainland were really getting most of its fish for *free*, because the islanders almost never redeemed their paper currency.

Every once in a while someone on the mainland would point out (with some alarm) that the islanders held a great deal of mainland currency and owned an ever-increasing amount of mainland real estate. So every few years the mainland would artificially devalue its paper currency. This was done, they would tell the islanders, to lower the price the island would pay for the mainland's products. But in actuality it had the effect of taking away much of the islanders hard-earned wealth, since all of the paper currency the islanders had accumulated was now worth only a fraction of what it was worth before. Moreover, every time the islanders purchased a piece of real estate on the mainland that started to increase in value, the local mainland government where the property was located increased the real estate taxes or prohibited the raising of rents—acts which the islanders were powerless to prevent, since their foreign real-estate investment on the mainland was subject to the laws of the mainland's local authorities.

As time went on some of the islanders began to get wise. They realized that their standard of living was far below that on the mainland, even though they were working twice as hard as mainland residents. But, as annoyed as they were, they couldn't see a way out. It seemed that their people just couldn't stop working; it was all they knew how to do. They hadn't developed much of an interest in recreational activities or much of an appetite for many of the things that the mainland produced, and they didn't know where to start. In the meantime, their elders continued to tax what they earned, refused to invest their taxes in projects to enhance the island instead of the mainland, and passed laws prohibiting the importation of the things the islanders wanted to purchase (like rice) from the mainland.

The island in this fable, of course, is the nation of Japan, and the mainland is the United States. And while the example may be a gross oversimplification of the relationship between the two countries, the principles are not that far from reality.

The simple reality is that the Japanese work much harder than Americans, and Americans reap the benefits. A Japanese citizen works more hours producing a less expensive but better quality product, which a U.S. citizen enjoys. The American uses the less expensive but better product, spends less time working and more time with his or her family, and spends the savings on the family's food, housing, and recreation. The paper money paid by the American to Japan for the product gets saved by the Japanese citizen in Japanese banks and pension funds, which recycle the money back to the United States by purchasing primarily assets that cannot be carried back to Japan, such as shares of stock in U.S. companies, U.S. treasury securities, and U.S. real estate.

The Japanese currently hold approximately $86 billion in U.S. treasury notes, representing about 22 percent of the $395 billion in U.S. debt held by foreigners.[14] This is probably the second worst investment they can make. U.S. treasury securities are not backed by any specific asset, such as gold, and thus their value can be artificially controlled by the U.S. government, which at any time can devalue its currency (by printing more money) to repay its debt. The value of any currency relative to another can fluctuate for a variety of reasons, but so long as the United States has a budget deficit and the Japanese continue to hoard rather than spend U.S. currency, one can be fairly sure that the dollar will be worth fewer yen each year. For example, suppose that a Japanese pension fund had purchased a $1,000 U.S. treasury security in 1985, when a U.S. dollar traded for 238.47 Japanese yen. To the Japanese workers who own the pension fund, that investment represented 238,470 yen. If the U.S. repaid that note in June 1988, when a dollar traded for 127.86 yen, the pension fund would have received 127,860 yen; only 54 percent of its original investment.

The Japanese worker, who must pay for his or her retirement in Japan with yen, not dollars, would have fared far better if the pension fund had invested in his or her own country. The investment would

[14]According to the Bureau of Public Debt in Washington, D.C. The total of $395 billion is from *The Budget of the United States Government Fiscal Year 1991* (Washington: Government Printing Office, 1990), A-97.

have remained stable in yen—the currency that is needed upon retirement; and the Japanese society would have reaped the benefit of that investment when the money was used to build badly needed Japanese sewers or transportation facilities. But investments of this type are virtually impossible on a large scale because the Japanese are generally paid for their products in dollars, not yen, which gives them no choice but to invest with the largest consumer of these dollars—the United States.

As stated above, U.S. treasury securities represent the second worst investment the Japanese can make. The worst possible investment they can make is U.S. real estate. In 1988, the Japanese purchased $16.54 billion worth of U.S. real estate.[15] The following year the Mitsubishi Estate Company purchased a majority interest in New York City's prestigious Rockefeller Center for $846 million.[16] This Rockefeller Center purchase followed numerous record-setting sales of prime U.S. office buildings to Japanese investors ranging from the Mitsui Real Estate Development's $610 million purchase of the Exxon Building in New York City to Shuwa Investment's $620 million purchase of ARCO Plaza in Los Angeles. The Japanese sun is also rising over the U.S. construction industry. In 1985 one Japanese company started construction on Hawaiian projects totaling more than $700 million, an enormous sum in a state where all nongovernment construction in that year totaled $862 million.[17]

Many people in the United States have wrongly interpreted these real estate investments as examples of Japanese economic superiority. The truth is that these investments are little more than cash gifts from the Japanese to the American people.

Most commercial real estate in the United States is owned by corporations that use it, or by U.S. pension funds and insurance companies that directly or indirectly invest in it.[18] As a result, local municipalities

---

[15]"Japanese to Keep Assets Flowing," *Pensions & Investment Age*, 1 May 1989, 15.

[16]James Sterngold, "Many Japanese Wary on Mitsubishi U.S. Deal," *New York Times*, 1 November 1989, D1.

[17]"I'll Take Manhattan—and Waikiki," *Time*, 9 March 1987, 62.

[18]Virtually all U.S. commercial real estate is either owned by these major financial institutions directly, or substantially owned through the form of long-term commercial mortgages (owned by these institutions) which receive the majority of the cash flow from the properties.

in need of money cannot simply raise the taxes on commercial real estate within their borders for two reasons. First, the entities that use and invest in the property are composed of domestic voters who will obviously not support the tax increase. Second, unless taxes remain competitive, those who use and invest in the property will leave the area.

However, when the Japanese have acquired a significant amount of U.S. real estate in a specific area—for example, downtown Los Angeles or Rockefeller Center—the local authorities will raise the real estate taxes on the property to provide additional funds to support local schools and services. The Japanese, as nonvoting U.S. investors, will be powerless to stop them. And while real estate owners can always threaten to pack up and leave, no one in the United States will be upset if the Japanese sell their U.S. real estate investments—at a fraction of what they paid for them—to U.S. investors who will then apply the necessary political muscle to get the taxes back in line.

In the 1980s, U.S. newspaper headlines frequently proclaimed that the Japanese were "buying up" America. Editorials decried this fact, and letters to the editor expressed the xenophobic fear of the average U.S. citizen that the United States would end up being "owned" by Japan. But these fears were unfounded because real estate in the United States, unlike investments in physical assets that can be carried away, is not an investment upon which the investor can exercise much control.

The owner of real estate in the United States is subject to local employment laws for the employees needed to work at the property, local zoning laws for the use that can be made of the property, local taxing authorities and utilities for how much can be earned from the property, and, perhaps most important, potential rent-control laws. Anyone considering the purchase of commercial real estate in the United States should have the ability to compete effectively in these political areas; indeed, such political control is often a prerequisite to a successful investment. And the simple fact of the matter is that, in this all-important arena, the Japanese can't compete for the simple reason that they don't vote.

But Japan's greatest problem is not the manner in which it has been investing its newfound manufacturing wealth. Nor is it the inefficiency of its economy, the spiraling price of its land, or the widening income distribution that is increasingly dividing it into a society of haves and have-nots. Japan's greatest problem is the very problem that caused the Great Depression of the 1930s: the Japanese people have not developed a desire to spend on themselves their newfound wealth. Indeed, this problem is so severe that it threatens to destroy the highly efficient manufacturing system on which virtually the entire Japanese economy rests.

In Chapter 3, Demand-Side Alchemy, we examined the driving force behind virtually the entire U.S. economy, namely alchemic demand or our endless appetite for goods and services above our basic needs. In the alchemic model, technology determines both the nature and level of consumer demand by determining what constitutes a need and the price at which goods or services can be sold. Moreover, individual consumer demand, even at a given level of technology, is virtually limitless because of the shift from quantity demand, the demand for more things, to quality demand, the demand for better things. This alchemic model contrasts with the classic Keynesian economic model, in which demand falls as income rises because as the consumer's basic needs are fulfilled he or she saves a greater percentage of income. The Keynesian model explained the cause of the Great Depression and offered a solution to it. However, today this model (as explained in Chapter 3) is obsolete; it does not explain or even describe our current U.S. alchemic economy.

The Japanese are not as fortunate when it comes to which economic model better explains their consumers' behavior. In contrast to Americans, the Japanese have behaved in a classic Keynesian fashion. Their overall consumption has *not* kept pace with their rising income. In the United States from 1980 to 1987, as real per capita GNP rose 24 percent, the ratio of savings to personal income declined from 7.1 to 3.7 percent; or, conversely, consumption rose from 92.9 to 96.3 percent. Quite contrary to Keynesian theory, the richer the average American became, the *higher* the proportion of income he or she consumed. But in Japan from 1980 to 1987, as real per capita GNP rose at approximately twice the rate of increase in the United States, the ratio of savings to personal income remained about the same, at a remarkably high 16 percent;[19] conversely, overall consumption remained stable at

---

[19]*Statistical Abstract of the United States 1989*, 436.

manufactured in the United States. The Japanese have transplanted more than 250 component-manufacturing firms to supply the automobile plants, and it is estimated that approximately 75 percent of the parts for Japan's domestically produced cars are made in the United States. A single Honda plant in Anna, Ohio, for example, produces components for at least 510,000 automobiles per year. In addition, most of the Japanese firms are establishing R & D facilities in the United States. (Mazda has a $23 million facility in California and Nissan has opened a $40 million research facility in Arizona.)[29]

While this transplant trend has just begun, major Japanese plants are also assembling everything from televisions to computers throughout North America in order to be physically closer to their American customer and his or her ever-changing demands. In Tijuana, Mexico, by 1987 Matsushita Electric was employing 2,000 Mexicans in eight plants to produce its Panasonic, Quasar, and Technics brands—and only six other Japanese companies accounted for 10 percent of the jobs in the more than 320 border-based assembly plants commonly known as *maquiladoras.*[30]

The economic impact of these transplants on the U.S. and Japanese economies is astounding. For example, the eight Japanese automobile transplants already in North America represent far more than an $8 billion gift from the Japanese to the American people. At a retail cost of only $10,000 per vehicle, the 2.26 million automobiles that these plants produce represent an *annual* addition of $22.6 billion dollars to the U.S. and Canadian economies. Even with no increase in the cars' sales price and the annual production level, these eight plants alone will contribute $226 to $452 billion to the U.S. and Canadian economies over the next ten to twenty years (the entire projected U.S. government deficit for 1990 was only $100 to 150 billion). And these contributions to our economy don't include the multiplier effect of the wages paid not only to the plants' 60,000 North American employees, but to the workers at the 250 component-assembly plants. In fact, except for the relatively small portion of profit that a transplant can export back to Japan, to a U.S. citizen there isn't much difference between a Honda

[29]Mair, Florida, and Kenney, "New Geography," 356–60.

[30]Joseph Contreras and John Schwartz, "The Far East Goes South," *Newsweek,* 22 June 1987, 46.

plant in Ohio and a Ford plant in Detroit except that the Honda plant exports 50,000 vehicles a year to Japan.

Far more significant than the positive impact that these Japanese-owned plants have on the U.S. economy is the negative effect that they have on the considerably smaller Japanese economy. Japan is roughly half the size of the United States in both population and economic wealth. Accordingly, a $22.6 billion per year positive impact on the United States has twice the negative impact on Japan. Put another way, if these transplants increase U.S. wealth by 2 percent, they decrease Japanese wealth by 4 percent. True, the Japanese do repatriate the profits from these plants in U.S. dollars (for eventual recycling to our economy); but these profits at most represent 10 percent of total sales and only 1 to 2 percent of the total economic benefit to the United States, when considering the multiplier effects of the monies paid to U.S. workers and suppliers.

The days are long gone when the Japanese could simply copy an existing U.S. product in a Japanese factory and then ship thousands of them to the United States at a lower price. And the days are almost gone when Japan can identify a demand for a product in the United States, design and manufacture it in Japan, and ship a still-competitive product back to the United States. Thus for the foreseeable future, in order to successfully compete for the U.S. and European customer in today's alchemic world, the Japanese will have to continue to export their capital—that is, their jobs and their best and brightest managers—to North America and Europe.

This simple reality bodes ill for Japan's citizens, for it is their future that is being sold by their country's multinational corporations in search of the almighty dollar. Perhaps never before have the legal free-market activities of private-sector organizations been so adverse to the interests of a free nation.

The answer to this predicament is not, as many have proposed, to legislate against Japanese foreign investment, either in Japan or in the United States. Rather, we must get the Japanese people—the people who created the production miracle of our age by turning their nation around after World War II—to begin enjoying the fruits of their labors. In other words, we must see that the Japanese people enter the demand-side of the alchemic age.

The Japanese have worked too hard and spent too little, and as a result have too much money. Moreover, the concept of "all work and no play" is beginning to take its toll on Japan's economy and its people. In 1990, the Japanese government reluctantly began a $2 million study to determine if hard work can be fatal. The study was prompted by a few lawsuits brought by families of *karoshi* (death from overwork) victims who successfully sued the government and certain companies for literally working their employees to death. Japanese office workers, for example, put in 500 more hours per year than their counterparts in West Germany and 225 more hours than Americans.[31]

But Japan's problems involve more than just overworked employees. The land-price spiral, which is widening existing class divisions in their society, is due as much to its citizens having hoarded too much money as it is to the shortage of land.

In response to the overabundance of hoarded money, the government has tried to induce its citizens to stop working so hard, but its efforts have so far met with limited success. In 1989, when banks closed on Saturdays as part of a nationwide move toward a five-day workweek, several prominent institutions let their employees know that they were expected to make up the lost time by working additional hours during the week.[32]

Unfortunately, the Japanese government is taking the wrong approach to the problem. Rather than induce its people to stop working so hard, the authorities should encourage the present work ethic and simultaneously help the Japanese develop interests that require the expenditure of money—interests which will enhance their life-styles and, more important, let their businesses go to work producing more products for their own people as well as for export. Such action will require a significant restructuring of their current political system, but it is an important step, for the current system impedes the natural creation of demand that is inherent in the alchemic process.

Most Americans enjoy the best life-style in the world today because they consume goods as efficiently as they produce them. In our alchemic world of unlimited resources, the strength of the U.S. economy

[31]David E. Sanger, "Tokyo Tries to Find Out if 'Salarymen' Are Working Themselves to Death," *New York Times*, 19 March 1990, A8.

[32]Sanger, "Tokyo Tries to Find Out," A8.

lies in our position as the world's leader in the demand for goods and services. Of course, as we saw in Chapter 3, this wasn't always so. An examination of consumer demand in America, relative to Japan, reveals the secrets behind the U.S. success and shows how Japan can learn from the American experience.

First, an American's single greatest incentive to spend money is the purchase of a private home. Home ownership not only has significant benefits for the individual (tax savings, better life-style, personal pride), it has a tremendous positive effect on the economy. The purchase of a home generates a series of fresh needs: new furniture, new carpet, new appliances, a new roof, a new coat of paint, even landscaping. The economy is stimulated as each of these needs is fulfilled, and the acquisition of each in turn creates another round of new demand. But in Japan, owing primarily to the political patronage accorded the farmers, home ownership is becoming increasingly difficult. And those Japanese who do manage to purchase homes find either that they are too small to allow room for furnishings or so expensive that there is little money left with which to buy them. Moreover, in the United States the federal government subsidizes the purchase of a new home, and local governments continually invest in upgrading the infrastructure that makes their residents' homes so attractive.[33] By contrast, the Japanese government has invested much of the country's extra wealth in the U.S. infrastructure rather than in its own. For example, to date Japan has purchased $86 billion of U.S. treasury securities and has invested a like amount in U.S. real estate, while it has "worse roads, sewers and parks than anywhere in Europe or North America."[34]

An American's second greatest incentive to spend money is the availability of an ever-increasing array of merchandise, offered each year at lower and lower prices. In America, competitively priced goods are produced and distributed for everyone, while in Japan, owing to the country's Byzantine distribution network, competitively priced goods

[33]U.S. citizens are allowed to deduct from their income taxes the costs of mortgage interest and property taxes paid on their primary residence, while in Japan government regulations, such as capital gains taxes of up to 94 percent and agricultural property tax rates that are one-tenth of residential rates, serve to keep housing and land prices artificially high. See James Sterngold, "While Land Prices in Japan Soar, Officials Fight Back With Words," *New York Times*, 24 March 1990, A1.

[34]Fallows, *More Like Us*, 42.

are produced and distributed for everyone *except* the Japanese. Moreover, the large chain retailers in the United States create demand through customer education and by offering a wide variety of choices. In Japan, by contrast, where there are few large chain retailers, these important components of alchemic demand—customer education and choice—are not well incorporated into the system.

In addition, goods that are not efficiently produced in America are imported, ensuring not only the best selection for U.S. citizens but also competition to keep the prices of U.S. producers in line. In Japan, imports are shunned, allowing both producers and distributors to extort outrageous prices from their own people for even basic staples. For example, the Japanese ban on rice imports costs Japanese consumers an estimated $28 billion. If only 10 percent of this market were opened to imports, it is estimated that the resulting lower prices would save Japanese consumers $6 billion a year.[35]

A third incentive to America's spending habits is the belief that there is nothing wrong with being individualistic and enjoying the fruits of your success. Indeed, Americans may well adhere to this view more strongly than any other people in the world. In Japan, however, there is a cultural bias toward conformity and against conspicuous consumption that goes back to the times of Buddha and Confucius. This is evident in the Japanese government's response to its citizens having hoarded too much money—that is, urging them to work less, rather than encouraging them to spend more.

In order for Japan to increase its internal demand for goods and services, it will be necessary to dismantle the government-sponsored exploitation of its citizens. But this will not come easily, since much of its political system is built upon the granting of economic favors to special-interest groups. It is ironic that the Japanese government—by preventing its own citizens from enjoying the fruits of their labors, by exporting its wealth in the form of lower priced products, and by investing overseas rather than domestically—is doing to its own people today what centuries of Japanese militarism had sought to do to neighboring countries.

However, as Japan is increasingly divided into a society of haves and

[35]Rahul Jacob, "Export Barriers the U.S. Hates Most," *Fortune*, 27 February 1989, 88.

have-nots, the seeds of political, and perhaps economic, reform are being planted. The rising land prices have "made the rich a lot richer and the poor more perceptive,"[36] causing the ruling Liberal Democratic party, which has traditionally catered to the politically powerful farmers, to begin openly debating agricultural land reform. And most recently a unprecedented wave of Japanese tourists traveling abroad is making them aware of how much less expensive even their own products are outside of Japan.

But looming much larger than social and political pressures for internal economic reform is the fact that, in the alchemic world, supply *follows* demand; to remain competitive in the fast-changing alchemic marketplace the Japanese manufacturing plants may have to follow their customers to Europe and America. Unless the Japanese can get their own house in order as a consuming nation, the Japanese multinational companies will continue to export their production capabilities, taking with them jobs, the best and brightest managers, and, ultimately, Japan's future as a nation.

Fortunately, Japanese yuppies have emerged, the so-called *shinjinrui*, or "new species," who to the traditional Japanese are "less interested in buckling down to work for the good of the nation than their parents were."[37] These hard-working, affluent, often two-career couples are more interested in spending their money than in endlessly saving it. And although they are currently shunned by the traditional Japanese as the potential end of the Japanese cultural past, they represent perhaps the sole hope for Japan's economic future.

[36]Lehner, "Disparities in Wealth," A1.

[37]"Is Japan as Rich as You Think?" *Newsweek*, 8 June 1987, 50.

CONCLUSION: THE AGE OF ALCHEMY

And God saw every thing that he had made, and, behold, it was very good.
—Genesis 1:31

LET'S REVIEW the Theory of Alchemy. At the heart of the theory is the First Law of Alchemy, which explains how technology defines a physical resource—for example, land was not a physical resource until people learned how to cultivate it.

The Second Law of Alchemy explains how the supply of physical resources is also determined by technology, because: (1) technology determines the efficiency with which we use our physical resources—for example, the fuel injector effectively doubled the supply of oil by doubling automobile gas mileage; and (2) technology determines our ability to find, obtain, distribute, and store physical resources—for example, the Alaska pipeline doubled the U.S. supply of oil.

The Third Law of Alchemy explains how the advance of technology is determined by the speed with which the members of a society exchange and process information. Each new advance in technology is the product of one or more other technological advances, and thus the speed with which people exchange and process information about their technological advances is the throttle controlling the overall advance

186

of technology. Moreover, technology has an exponential relationship upon itself—that is, advances in technology multiply upon each other as each technological advance leads directly to new technological advances.

These first three laws constitute Supply-Side Alchemy and lead us to the central formulation of alchemic theory, $W = PT^n$, where wealth equals physical resources multiplied by technology, and technology has an exponential relationship upon itself.

In conventional economic theories, wealth is a function of only physical resources because technology is considered to be constant over a person's lifetime and thus not part of the decision-making process. In alchemic theory, technology is considered to be dynamic over a person's lifetime and, because of its exponential relationship upon itself, is the most important component in determining overall wealth. Thus while conventional economic theories are primarily concerned with how to maximize value by efficiently distributing a fixed supply of wealth, the Theory of Alchemy is primarily concerned with how to maximize value by creating and distributing more wealth.

As long as there is an abundance of technology, as there is in the world today, there is an abundance of physical resources or wealth. However, an abundance of technology does not ensure that people will have everything they want. In the alchemic world, as explained by the Fourth and Fifth Laws of Alchemy which constitute Demand-Side Alchemy, the only thing growing faster than our supply of goods and services is our demand for them.

The Fourth Law of Alchemy explains how there is an unlimited demand for products and services because technology determines what constitutes a need. This law is entirely analogous to the role of technology on the supply side. Automobiles, better clothing, electronics, and virtually 95 percent of the things we "need" today are items whose demand was created by technology.

The Fifth Law of Alchemy explains how technology determines the level of demand for existing goods and services by determining the price at which they can be sold. As the price goes down, the demand goes up, and in the alchemic world demand is unlimited because of the shift from quantity demand to quality demand. For example, as the price of a suit goes down, a person will purchase an increased quantity of suits, along with more ties, shirts, and shoes to match. And when he has all the suits he wants, he will probably switch to a better quality suit, along with better quality ties, shirts and shoes, starting the process all over again.

Virtually the whole of our modern economy is built upon Demand-Side Alchemy. If it weren't, Supply-Side Alchemy's ability to provide everyone with everything he or she needs (for basic survival) would cause our economy to grind to a halt. Moreover, because we can effectively produce with technology virtually everything we demand, it is our demand for goods and services that determines what will be supplied in our alchemic world.

Once we realize that technology controls nearly all economic activity, the most important question becomes, what can predict the immediate growth of technology for an individual, an industry, or a society? This is explained by the Sixth Law of Alchemy, which explains the technology gap—the difference between the best practices possible with current knowledge and the practices actually in use. The technology gap is the sum of the Ready-to-be-Implemented Technological advances *(R-I-Ts)* that we haven't yet utilized. In order for an R-I-T to be literally "ready to be implemented," it must be user transparent—that is, it must not require any more skills from the user than the product it is meant to replace. Examples of R-I-Ts include radial tires that haven't yet replaced standard bias-ply models and electric typewriters that haven't yet replaced manual ones.

Using the Theory of Alchemy we have examined our lives, our jobs, our educational systems, our children, our immigrants, and our most important trading partner, Japan. We have seen how the Theory of Alchemy can explain our past, help us live in the present, and predict our future. But far more important than predicting our future, the Theory of Alchemy can be used to *shape* it.

We saw in Chapter 5 that in today's alchemic world our labor supply is our capital supply. And unlike throughout most of human history, what mainly determines the value of a person's labor is how much he or she is willing to invest in education and training. Since by and large most people today have the freedom to further their education and training, and thereby enhance their worth in the labor force, the Age of Alchemy might also be called the Age of Autonomy.

In Chapter 6 and Chapter 7 we used the Theory of Alchemy to understand why the benefits of our alchemic age are not being enjoyed by everyone in our society, and we examined what we can do to get more of our citizens on the alchemic train to success. In Chapter 8 we discovered that our immigrants are making us richer, not the other way around.

Throughout Chapters 6 through 8 it was comforting to see that in the Age of Alchemy, where one person's gain is not another person's loss, what we believe we should do because it is morally right is also exactly what we should do to selfishly increase our individual wealth.

In Chapter 9 we learned how the United States surpassed Great Britain as an industrial power by developing better ways of managing technological resources, and then how Japan, fifty years later, similarly passed the United States. But, as we saw in Chapter 10, the Japanese haven't developed the internal demand for goods and services on which an alchemic economy is based. As a result, the Japanese are not enjoying the fruits of their labors and are entirely dependent on foreign powers for their economic well-being.

The U.S. economy has enjoyed nearly a decade of unprecedented economic prosperity. In 1987, when the current economic expansion passed its fifth consecutive year—at the time, the longest expansionary period in our history—there were many who, using conventional economic theories, predicted that the inevitable crash was just around the corner. Indeed, the best-selling book of 1987 was called *The Great Depression of 1990*. Today, we know that nothing could be further from the truth.

An Alchemist would have been able to see, back in 1981, that owing to an ever-widening technology gap, the United States—and the entire Western World—was entering a multidecade period of expansion of unfathomable proportions. Today we are not even through the first decade. Let's now examine how the Theory of Alchemy can explain more of what is happening to our total economic picture as we enter the final years of the twentieth, or alchemic, century.

In January of 1981, when Ronald Reagan was inaugurated as president, the total federal debt was approximately $908 billion. The budget deficit that year—the difference between how much money the government takes in and how much it spends each year—was approximately $74 billion, causing the total federal debt to rise to $982 billion. During the next eight years the *annual* budget deficit rose as high as $238 billion, and by the end of the Reagan administration the total federal debt had reached $2,600 billion.[1]

Throughout the last decade the budget deficit and the resulting federal debt was the major financial issue in U.S. politics. In the election year of 1988, Americans were told that the seemingly unlimited prosperity most of them had been experiencing was the result of borrowing $1,692 billion during the Reagan years; that we had been "mortgaging our future" by spending above our means; and that we were leaving the debt as a terrible legacy to our descendants. This was one of the most specious claims made in the 1988 presidential campaign, yet even the winner, George Bush, was elected in part because he made the strongest case against the dire consequences that awaited us if we did not reduce the spiraling federal debt.

The truth is that in the alchemic world, the federal debt, estimated to reach $3,319 billion by the end of 1991, is among the least significant of our concerns. It might become significant over time if rising budget deficits remain unchecked, but it certainly isn't a critical issue now and won't be for the next decade. Here's why.

Consider the following: A man with an annual income of $100,000 from his business, projected to increase approximately 4 percent or $4,000 per year, owns a home worth more than $1 million on which he has a $56,000 mortgage. His annual mortgage interest payments total $5,600. He comes to ask you, a professional financial adviser, for advice.

It seems that in addition to a handicapped child who requires special schooling, the man has two children about to enter college and needs an additional $2,500 a year to ensure that all his children receive a proper education. He has considered cutting back on the amount of money he reinvests each year in his business, but has been advised that taking out an additional $2,500 a year from the business would jeopardize the business' projected 4 percent annual growth rate. He is already counting on the $4,000 per annum projected annual growth rate in his income to meet rising living and educational expenses for his family. His banker has agreed to let him defer $2,500 of his $5,600 mortgage interest each year and add the deferred amount to the principal,

---

[1]*Economic Report of the President February 1990* (Washington: Government Printing Office, 1990), 383.

thereby increasing the mortgage balance by $2,500 annually. He doesn't know when he will be able to resume making the full mortgage payments, and wants your advice as to how long he should continue deferring the interest before worrying that his mortgage balance is too high.

Since, as a rule of thumb, home mortgage payments should not exceed 25 percent of household income, you tell him that so long as he earns $100,000 per year, his mortgage balance can rise to $250,000 (requiring annual interest payments of $25,000) before he should be concerned. Deferring $2,500 of his interest payments each year, it would take twenty-eight years, including interest on his deferred interest, for his mortgage balance to reach this $250,000 level. Thus you explain to him that he has at least twenty-eight years before financial prudence would require he begin making his full payments. (In addition, you point out that his $100,000 annual income, if it continues growing at 4 percent per year, will be $300,000 per annum in twenty-eight years, which would justify a mortgage balance then of $750,000.)

This example is analogous to our present situation concerning the federal debt and deficit. It is estimated that in 1991 the federal deficit will be $141 billion, the federal debt will be $3,319 billion, and GNP will be $5,892 billion. The $141 billion federal deficit is to the $3,319 billion federal debt, about 4 percent, exactly what the $2,500 mortgage payment deferral is to the $56,000 home mortgage. And the $3,319 billion debt is to the $5,892 billion GNP about 56 percent, what the $56,000 mortgage balance is to the man's $100,000 annual income. (GNP is currently growing at 7 percent per annum.)[2]

Certainly, we should always focus on how much our government spends and what it does with our tax dollars. But quite contrary to what many of our politicians would have us believe, we are not going to fall off the economic edge of the world if we do not immediately begin massively cutting our federal budget. In fact, the only way we might fall off the economic edge is if we *do* immediately begin massively cutting social and reinvestment programs critical to our long-term growth.

---

[2]These numbers are not adjusted for inflation because they are being compared to the federal debt which is held in dollars that are depreciating owing to inflation. Real (adjusted for inflation) GNP is still growing at 2 to 3 percent per year.

In a book published in 1986, David Stockman, the first director of the Office of Management and Budget in the Reagan administration, explained how various elected officials thwarted his efforts to massively cut the federal budget.[3] Stockman was convinced that unless the budget was balanced immediately, inflation and interest rates would soon exceed 20 percent, GNP would begin to decline, and the country would begin an economic downturn that could rival the Great Depression. Of course, we know today that Stockman was mistaken. Despite his dire predictions, over the next three years while the budget deficit and the federal debt rose unchecked, GNP continued its meteoric rise, inflation fell to its lowest levels since the 1960s,[4] and interest rates fell more than 50 percent to their lowest levels since the 1970s.[5] Stockman, blinded by his belief that the federal budget must be cut, titled his book *The Triumph of Politics*, in sarcastic reference to the success of elected officials in thwarting his efforts. It should have been titled *The Triumph of Democracy*, in deference to the many politicians who, successfully representing their constituents, were able to retain many important social programs that otherwise would have been cut. In fact, an alchemic analysis of the past ten years would call for a *doubling* of the federal debt, even if we could only ensure that we would get half the return on our investment that we did during that time. Here's why.

In 1981 the gross national product of the United States—the indicator that most accurately reflects our wealth—was $2,986 billion, or approximately $12,975 for every person in the country. By 1989, GNP had risen to $5,151 billion, or $20,705 per person. During eight Reagan years the federal government borrowed an additional $1,692 billion, but our nation's *annual* gross national product increased by an unbelievable $2,165 billion. In individual terms, during these eight years the total federal debt rose $6,801 per person, but total output rose $8,703 per person. Thus, looking at the federal budget alone, we invested

[3]David A. Stockman, *The Triumph of Politics* (New York: Avon Books, 1986).

[4]Inflation, measured by changes in the consumer price index for all items, fell to 1.1 percent in 1986 and averaged approximately 4 percent for the rest of the decade. Inflation did average approximately 3.35 percent for a brief period during the Nixon administration (1971–1972) but this was due primarily to artificial wage-and-price controls which were recovered in the record-setting inflation levels of 8.7 and 12.3 percent in 1973 and 1974. See *Economic Report of the President February 1990*, 363.

[5]*Economic Report of the President February 1990*, 376.

$6,801 billion over eight years and reaped an unbelievable *128 percent* on our investment. Even looking (more accurately) at total debt for all sectors of the economy—federal, state, consumer, and business—our return on investment is still several times each year's cost of servicing and repaying the total debt.

What happened, as explained in Chapter 1, is that in 1981 America began to retool its productive capacity in an alchemic age, causing an unprecedented increase in productivity that led to the incredible 72 percent (24 percent after adjusting for inflation) increase in GNP by 1988. The numbers, shown in the table that follows, speak for themselves:[6]

Year	Gross National Product (billions)	GNP (per capita)	Total Employment (thousands)	Unemployment Rate (%)
1981	$2,986	$12,982	100,397	7.5
1982	$3,139	$13,500	99,526	9.5
1983	$3,322	$14,148	100,834	9.5
1984	$3,688	$15,562	105,005	7.4
1985	$3,952	$16,516	107,150	7.1
1986	$4,181	$17,304	109,597	6.9
1987	$4,430	$18,161	112,440	6.1
1988	$4,792	$19,454	114,968	5.4
1989	$5,151	$20,705	117,342	5.2

NOTE: GNP in 1990 and 1991 is projected to be $5,489 and $5,892 billion, respectively.

However, if these numbers reflect such a dramatic increase in our country's wealth, why is it that so many of us don't feel rich? The answer for most of us, as explained in Chapter 3, is that the only thing rising faster than our actual physical wealth is our expectations. However for some of us, physical wealth has been steadily declining.

The grim reality of our alchemic age is that while our total wealth is growing at an unprecedented pace, our rich are getting richer and our poor are getting poorer. And despite the many claims to the contrary, the explanation behind this increasing bifurcation has very little to do with politics. What was happening in the 1980s, as explained in Chapters 5, 6, and 7, was that more and more of our citizens

[6]*Economic Report of the President February 1990,* 383, 329, 332, 338.

shops. In fact, the majority of the large parts used by collision repair shops may come from stolen vehicles.[9] (This was well-illustrated by the T-top craze in the 1980s when auto owners seeking to purchase replacements for their stolen T-top roof panels, created an ever-spiraling demand for more roof panels, which in turn led to more stolen roof panels.)

Rather than deal with the cause of motor vehicle theft—the demand for parts—we have developed an economic solution that benefits only our middle- and upper-class citizens. Our automobile insurance system simply reimburses the middle- and upper-class drivers for the value of their stolen vehicles, effectively legitimizing automobile theft. But the poor, who cannot afford theft insurance, often face severe economic problems when their vehicles are stolen. And the system perpetuates itself because each year, as more automobiles are stolen, the insurance companies maintain their profit margins simply by raising their premiums to cover their increased expenses.

In addition to the insurance companies, automobile manufacturers and retailers benefit from motor-vehicle theft, although at a much larger cost to society. The 1.3 million annual victims of motor-vehicle theft represent a significant portion of the approximately 10 million annual purchasers of new motor vehicles. Indeed, an auto dealer's best customer may be a victim who has just received a check from his or her insurance company and needs an immediate replacement for the stolen vehicle.

Here's how an Alchemist would solve the problem of motor-vehicle theft. In the alchemic world virtually everything, including property crime, is driven by demand. Therefore, the Alchemist would concentrate on *reducing the demand* for stolen vehicles, rather than on reducing the seemingly endless supply of auto thieves. This could be done as follows:

Insurance companies would not pay for any collision repair unless the invoice from the body shop contained a certificate of origin for all parts

---

[9]This statement comes from conversations with owners of collision repair shops who often cannot find legitimate channels to purchase certain parts for body repair. It would be relatively easy to determine the depth of this problem by comparing insurance claims paid for certain parts, say the rear bumper of a 1990 Cadillac Seville, with the number of additional bumpers actually manufactured, and the number of stolen un-recovered 1990 Cadillac Sevilles.

costing more than $100. This would force the body shops to ensure the legitimacy of their purchases, virtually eliminating the market for stolen vehicles.

This type of private sector solution to a public problem was accomplished earlier in this century when every state in the nation, working with the automobile manufacturers, implemented a system of government automobile registration using vehicle identification numbers (VINs). The VIN, which is permanently engraved on all automobiles sold in the United States, has virtually eliminated the domestic market for whole (that is, nondisassembled) stolen vehicles by eliminating the demand for them; no one wants to purchase a motor vehicle that cannot be registered. (The few stolen vehicles that are not disassembled are shipped overseas intact.) It is time to implement a similar system to eliminate the market for stolen automobile parts.

In addition, automobile manufacturers should be fined based on a weighted percentage of their vehicles that are stolen relative to those of other manufacturers. This would encourage manufacturers to develop better antitheft and parts-registration systems.[10] It is absurd that we currently tax manufacturers whose vehicles have much greater than average fuel consumption, but we don't tax manufacturers whose vehicles have higher than average rates of theft. The cost to society of a stolen automobile is far greater than the cost of below-average fuel economy.

But the real tragedy in our having effectively legitimized motor-vehicle theft is what it has done to increase the bifurcation of our society. The percentage of black citizens touched by automobile theft is 162 percent that of whites.[11] We have built an insurance system that covers the costs of property crime for the middle and upper classes but leaves the poor to suffer the financial burden of their loss. We must get the insurance companies to confront the problem directly, rather than merely pass the cost of property theft on to the insured.

The third area where we have unsuccessfully tried economic rather

[10]In the 1960s, ignition systems were developed that locked the steering wheel when the key was removed, reducing the incidence of automobile theft for "joy rides."

[11]In 1987, 2.3 per thousand black households experienced a motor vehicle theft, as compared to 1.4 per thousand for white households and 1.5 per thousand for all U.S. households. See *Statistical Abstract of the United States 1989*, 171.

than alchemic solutions is the number one problem facing America today: illegal drugs.

The retail value of the illegal drug business in the United States today is estimated to be as high as $120 billion a year. When lost productivity, treatment programs, and crime are considered, the cost to society of the illicit drug trade is at least several times this amount. Eliminating or sharply reducing illegal drug use in the United States would likely yield the greatest economic benefit of any government program, existing or proposed.

Unfortunately, the U.S. government has consistently tried an economic rather than an alchemic solution to this critical problem, with limited or no success. From 1981 to 1991 the portion of the federal budget devoted to eliminating illegal drug use rose almost linearly from $1.4 to $10.6 billion, virtually all of it aimed at curbing the *supply of* rather than the *demand for* illegal drugs.[12] This is alchemically foolish and socially dangerous.

It is foolish to try to control the supply of illegal drugs because in our alchemic world, where the market has no corners, as long as there is a demand for a product some smart (although in this case illegal) Alchemist is going to find a way to fill it. Indeed, the supply of illegal drugs is as well explained by the Second Law of Alchemy as is any other product: the supply of a specific resource is determined by technology in two ways—first by the efficiency of its use; and second, by our ability to find and distribute it. The cocaine industry has used technology to increase the efficiency of the drug to the point where a user can experience the same high from a $5 rock of crack as he or she formerly got from a $100 gram of cocaine.[13] On the distribution side, every time our government succeeds in stopping one country from producing or

[12]The 1991 figure of $10.6 billion represents a 1990 administration budget proposal rather than actual outlays. See *Budget of the United States Government Fiscal Year 1991* (Washington: Government Printing Office, 1990), 111.

[13]It is ironic that while the administration's 1990 National Drug Control Strategy is virtually entirely devoted to eliminating the supply of rather than the demand for illegal drugs, its 1990 report acknowledges that the technology of drug supply is rapidly evolving from cocaine to crack and now to "ice," a smokeable crystallized form of methamphetamine from Asia that produces up to an eight-hour high (versus twenty minutes for crack) and is already becoming the "drug of choice" in Hawaii. See *National Drug Control Strategy* (Washington: Government Printing Office, January 1990), 45.

distributing illegal drugs, another country appears to take its place. Our battle to control the supply of drugs is analogous to Hercules' attempt to defeat the multiheaded Hydra—every time he crushed one of the Hydra's heads, two heads arose in its place.

Moreover, serious attempts to control the supply of drugs are socially dangerous. In a free society there is no way to control the supply of anything people demand without risking the very liberties that make the society free. Only a totalitarian regime could control supply, and even then only for relatively short periods of time (or, more likely, until the regime self-destructed). Thus while it is laudable for the government to pursue those who supply illegal drugs, such efforts, however successful, will not solve the problem. *The only way to solve the drug problem in our alchemic world is to reduce the demand for illegal drugs.* Here's a suggested approach.

Despite all the attention paid by the media to the crack-using, inner-city, minority-group drug addict, the overwhelming majority of the annual $120 billion illegal drug purchases in this country are made by white middle- and upper-class Americans who buy primarily marijuana and cocaine for recreational use. Sales of crack (at $5 a rock) may outnumber sales of cocaine (at $100 a gram) or marijuana (at $75 an ounce), but there is simply not enough money in the inner-city segment of the business to support the present drug trade, an international infrastructure that rivals in power and technology the best and largest multinational corporations.[14] Thus, despite the media's focus on the inner-city addict, it is the relatively affluent middle-class user on whom the survival of the illegal drug trade depends. If we can eliminate or greatly reduce the demand for illegal drugs among these millions of recreational users, the drug-dealing infrastructure, unable to support itself on sales to inner-city addicts, will disappear.[15]

While science and medical technology have not yet provided a

[14]Indeed, the total combined household income (after taxes) of every one of the 10,736,000 black and 4,085,000 Hispanic households in America ($163.3 billion and $67.2 billion in 1987, respectively) does not equal much more than the total amount spent in the U.S. on illegal drugs. See *Statistical Abstract of the United States 1989*, 440–444.

[15]It should be noted that while the inner-city addicts support their drug habits primarily through property theft, they themselves only receive a small percentage of what we think the value of these stolen items is when they sell them to buy drugs.

means to control illegal drug use by the true addict, we do have the technology to control illegal drug use by recreational users. Moreover, since virtually all drug addicts began as recreational users, the elimination of recreational drug use would effectively stop new people from becoming drug addicts.

The Fifth Law of Alchemy explains how technology determines the level of demand for existing goods and services by determining the price at which they can be sold. It is time to reduce the level of demand for recreational drugs among our middle- and upper-class citizens by drastically increasing their price. Here's how to do it, alchemically.

First, every state, county, city, town, and village should immediately pass legislation taxing each ounce of marijuana $750 and each gram of cocaine $2,000. Then, to ensure payment of the tax, the authorities should be empowered to confiscate private property in or on which any untaxed substance is found until the tax is paid. For example, if the police found two ounces of marijuana in a teenager's BMW, regardless of who in the car possessed the drug, they would impound the vehicle until the $1,500 tax was paid. If three grams of cocaine were found in a home or apartment, a lien would be put on the property or its possessions until the $6,000 tax was paid. As a result, drug use would no longer be tolerated by the families or friends of users, because these otherwise innocent people would suffer significant financial hardship if drugs were found on their property.

The police, upon discovering illegal drugs, would be able to make arrests for tax evasion as well as for possession. Those arrested could be tried in a separate court system, the cost of which would be paid with the taxes and penalties collected. These tax charges would be separate from criminal charges which could also be imposed.

The most important feature of this program would be an amnesty option, allowing any first-time offender to pay a greatly reduced tax and be cleared of any criminal charges. The accused person electing the amnesty option would confess to the charge of possession, pay only 10 percent of the normal tax ($75 per ounce of marijuana and $200 per gram of cocaine), attend a six-month drug education program similar to driver-education programs for traffic violators, and be placed on probation for thirty-six months. All charges would be dropped and all records of the arrest expunged, provided the person avoided the use, possession, and presence of illegal drugs during the probationary period. A violation of the terms of probation would subject the person to the balance of the tax they did not pay, as well as to the criminal charges for possession to which they would have already signed a confession.

In addition, a modified amnesty option would be available for the person who is medically or self-identified as an addict rather than as a recreational user. Such a person would be enrolled in a drug-treatment program, paid for in part by the confessed addict (based on his financial resources) and in part by the taxes collected from the recreational users. Successful completion of the treatment program would entitle the person to participate in the amnesty option described above. Failure to complete the program successfully would subject the person to liability for the originally brought tax and criminal charges.

One of the major benefits of this program is how quickly it could be implemented on a local level without requiring national legislation. Each municipality would have the freedom to tailor the program to suit the particular needs and tastes of its citizens. Once implemented, the program would make communities virtually drug free by eliminating the drug dealer's major customers. The dealers, left without buyers to support their illicit trade, would have no choice but to move to another area.

We must implement such a program quickly. Many otherwise fine, upstanding citizens are recreational drug users who are totally ignorant of what their habit costs society. These citizens are generally unaware that their money buys weapons that are used to murder law-enforcement officers; that it supports dealers who supply drugs to our children; and that it fosters the ever-increasing crime plaguing us today. The alchemic solution to the problem of illegal drugs is simple; we need only act to implement it.

The fourth area where there is an alchemic solution to a seemingly complex problem is in making decent housing affordable for every U.S. family. For years the cost of many common consumer items, such as automobiles, televisions, and food, has been falling. But the median price of a new, single-family home rose from $48,800 in 1977 to $104,500 in 1987, pricing the classic American dream out of the reach of tens of millions of families.[16] And we have only ourselves to blame, because our local political system, exercising control over the home-

[16]The median price of existing (not new) single-family houses rose during this period from $42,900 to $85,900, paralleling the rise in the price of new construction. See *Statistical Abstract of the United States 1989*, 702.

building industry, has prevented the Theory of Alchemy from working to lower prices.

It is estimated that local building codes, which vary widely from community to community, add between 30 and 50 percent to the cost of a new home. This increased cost lies not in the existence of such codes (which certainly perform a worthwhile function), but in the fact that each community has a *different* code. The absence of a uniform set of building regulations fragments the market, hindering the implementation of innovations that would lower prices.[17]

The Theory of Alchemy is able to solve our problems in the automobile industry because a manufacturer who comes up with a new idea need only submit it to one federal agency for approval, upon receipt of which he or she can market the concept throughout the country. By contrast, a manufacturer who comes up with an innovative new method for home construction, such as a new plumbing or electrical system, would have to comply with the different requirements of literally thousands of building codes in our cities, towns, and villages in order to market it nationally. If building codes were uniform in their requirements—even for electrical, plumbing, and framing requirements only—several enterprising companies would do for houses what Ford did for automobiles, changing home builders into home manufacturers. (Think what the price of an automobile would be if manufacturers had to comply with *different* safety and pollution requirements for each state, let alone each town, in which their vehicles were sold.) A uniform national building code could reduce the cost of new construction by up to 50 percent, making the American dream a reality for tens of millions of families.

Communities often use building codes to protect their local trade unions and to keep home prices artificially high in order to maintain the exclusivity of particular neighborhoods. Thus the actions of our local governments, selfishly seeking to protect the value of existing homes, and the inaction of our federal government, which has yet to pass national legislation to help those citizens unable to afford the American dream, have kept the alchemic process from naturally working in the home-building industry.

[17]It is also argued that many local trade unions perpetuate this system in order to protect the jobs of their members.

The fifth area we will consider, in which we have not let the alchemic process take its natural course, is environmental pollution. The Second Law of Alchemy explains how the level of technology determines our supply of an already-defined resource. So how is it that in this age of unlimited technology we seem to be depleting our two most important resources, clean air and clean water? The answer is that we have not applied alchemic theory to the consumption of air and water. We should charge a fair price for all air and water used (or destroyed), and then let the smart Alchemists among us determine ways to efficiently control their use.

For example, every automobile should be taxed based upon the amount of oxygen it consumes and the volume and purity of the exhaust it emits. This would force both manufacturers and consumers to view environmental protection prospectively—in making production and purchase decisions—rather than retrospectively—in the form of fines or additional taxes which are often arbitrarily imposed and usually penalize companies and people for something they were not aware of at the time they did it.

Our objective in briefly examining these five areas—the minimum wage, automobile theft, illegal drugs, affordable housing, and environmental pollution—has been to illustrate how seemingly unsolvable problems become manageable when viewed under the alchemic microscope. In today's alchemic world, where wealth is a function not of scarce physical resources but of seemingly unlimited technology, the problems that remain are the problems for which we have not yet developed and applied alchemic solutions.

When I first moved my real estate business to Texas in 1981, I had the pleasure of dealing with several wealthy and powerful families and individuals—the Hunts, the Murchisons, former Governor John Connally, and others—most of whom had acquired their wealth over successive generations. Over the next five years I watched in horror as these families—and hundreds of other individuals, many of them close friends—lost everything they had. They had to explain to their families why their homes were on the market, explain to their children why they could no longer attend private school, and explain to the merchants and business partners who had trusted them why they could no longer meet their financial obligations.

What happened to these Texans in the 1980s, and is presently happening to millions of Americans every day, is well explained by the Theory of Alchemy. Each of these people, seeking to store their wealth for the benefit of the people they loved, invested in physical assets— land, minerals, stocks, bonds, and so on. But in the alchemic world, where the value of every physical asset is determined by ever-changing technology, there is no place to simply *store* wealth. *In the Alchemic world, there is no absolute store of value.*

As discussed in Chapter 2, there are two types of value in the alchemic world: the traditional market (or speculative) value, and the alchemic fundamental productive value. The market (or speculative) value of an item is what someone is willing to pay for it. The value of a painting, an ounce of gold, or shares of stock are all determined in this fashion. But such speculative demand is very fickle. A piece of land worth $10 million one day because a developer proposes to build a regional shopping center on it might be worth only $100,000 the next day when the developer decides to build on land a few miles away.

The alchemic fundamental productive value of an item is its price relative to another item that can be substituted for it—for example, the price of oil relative to coal or natural gas. Holding technology constant, this is the lowest price an item should fall to, because below this value some smart Alchemist will start purchasing the commodity and substituting it for another item. But in the alchemic world we *cannot* hold technology constant. It is technology—more than the supply of or the demand for an item, and even more than the price of a substitute—that determines fundamental productive value. This applies not only to traditional commodities but to investments in income-producing businesses and real estate as well.

For example, the fundamental productive value of a shopping center is determined by the amount of merchandise it distributes to consumers, as measured by the total retail sales generated by the stores inside. Today, retail sales average between $100 and $150 per square foot of shopping-center space. But most of the new retailers—mass-market superstores specializing in electronics, discount clothes, toys, and the like—average sales of $300 to $450 per square foot. These new retailers, utilizing the latest computer technology for sales and inventory control, are selling three times the number of goods in the same amount of floor space as the average retailer. Their increased sales, which they accomplish by offering a greater selection of merchandise at lower prices, come at the expense of smaller, less-efficient competitors who soon have no choice but to close their doors.

These new retailers have found a way to distribute the merchandise our country wants in roughly one-third the shopping-center space now occupied by the entire retail industry. As a result, we may soon need only one-half to one-third of our existing 3.7 billion square feet of retail space. This has created a fast-paced game of musical chairs in the retail industry, as each shopping center owner tries to ensure that its shopping center will be leased to these new, high-sales tenants when the music finally stops.[18] (Incidentally, I have no doubt that when it does stop some smart Alchemist will find a use for much of the vacant shopping-center space, perhaps as child-care centers.)

Alchemic investors in shopping centers, industrial buildings, and even apartments know that the ability of management to attract and keep top tenants is as or more important than the physical asset itself. This was explained in the first article I wrote related to the Theory of Alchemy, titled "The Real Estate Business and Technological Obsolescence."[19] The article examined how the traditional maxim of the three most important things in real estate investing—"location, location, and location"—has given way to three more important criteria—"information, information, and information."

Technology today is what makes one individual's earning power a thousand times that of another; it is what makes companies that work with information far more valuable than those that work with physical resources; and it is what gives a country like Japan, with few physical resources, one of the world's highest per capita GNPs. (Conversely, it is the lack of technology that gives a country like the Soviet Union, with the most physical resources, one of the lowest per capita GNPs).

Technology not only determines the value of physical resources or stores of value, *technology itself is perhaps the only store of value.* The value of an individual, a company, and even a country is its level of

[18]In actuality, the prognosis for the shopping-center industry is even worse when one considers the effect of overnight delivery services and direct manufacturer-to-customer sales.

[19]Paul Zane Pilzer, "The Real Estate Business and Technological Obsolescence," *Real Estate Review* (Fall 1989): 30–33.

technology. The best way for an individual to store wealth today is to improve his or her basic skills; the way for a society to store wealth today is to improve the basic skills level of its citizens. In a traditional economic environment, capital—already-produced goods that are used in the production of other goods—is an excellent store of value. In our alchemic environment, where labor is capital, improving the educational level of our citizens may be the only long-term way to store value.

No traditional store of value, even money, is insulated from the impact of alchemic change. A person who put $10,000 in a newborn child's college education trust fund in 1968 found that eighteen years later the $10,000 was worth, in 1968 purchasing power, only $3,175. The $10,000 would have had to grow to $31,496 just to keep up with inflation.

This bodes ill for those individuals who passively store their wealth, but it bodes well for society as a whole. It forces every member of our society who has accumulated capital to constantly seek out the best investment opportunities, for the only guarantee in today's market is the assurance that you will lose if you sit still. This accounts for much of the growth of our financial services industry, and benefits our economy by providing a virtually limitless supply of capital for innovative ideas, whether they come from the corporate board room or the college classroom.[20]

In analyzing any potential investment opportunity, when we apply the six laws of the Theory of Alchemy we usually see initially surprising, but then surprisingly obvious, results. In Chapter 2 we examined how the distribution versus the accumulation of resources will be a key component in investing in the 1990s. In Chapter 3 we saw how the development of new products and ideas, rather than the control of existing products or technologies that were once thought to have a corner on their markets, is the only way to stay ahead—or even stay even—in our fast-changing alchemic marketplace. And, most important, in Chapter 4 we saw how the ever-changing technology gap can be used to predict what is going to happen next on both the supply and demand sides of the economic equation.

[20]Today, it is easier than ever to start a new business. Thanks to our cutting-edge financial services industry, virtually everything needed can be financed or leased. Almost anything—from restaurant ovens to office equipment—can be obtained from a specialty firm that will finance it, and, for a price, take it back if it is no longer needed.

Thus if you are rich today, in order to remain so you must keep abreast of alchemic changes as you continually decide where to *temporarily* store your wealth. And the only way to keep abreast of alchemic changes is to constantly search for the best investment opportunities; today these lie not in purchasing static commodities, but in training people and developing new ideas.

In 1798, the economist Thomas Malthus argued that the working class was doomed to live in misery because its birth rate would always increase in proportion to its rising affluence.[21] At a natural increase rate of 3 percent a year, a society's population will double every twenty-three years, doubling the number of people who must share what was thought to be a fixed supply of physical resources. No wonder Malthus regarded war, famine, and pestilence as "positive checks" on population growth.

But Malthus didn't foresee that, as a result of technology, economic output would far outstrip the 3 percent population growth rate (U.S. real GNP rose 24 percent from 1981 to 1988 while population, including at least 5 million new immigrants, rose only 7 percent).[22] Moreover, he didn't foresee the invention of the birth control pill and that millions of families would voluntarily elect to control their own population growth. It appears, therefore, that Malthus missed the boat. Or did he?

An alchemic economic forecast today would project that the real growth rate in world GNP for each of the next few decades will equal or exceed even the salubrious 1980s—even though world population is only expected to roughly double during the entire twenty-first century to about 10 billion people. But virtually all of this projected economic growth will be in the *developed* nations of the world, which are experiencing little or no increase in their population. Virtually all of the projected population growth will be in the less-developed or Third World nations, which are experiencing little or no economic growth. Let's examine why this is so.

First, the most effective product for controlling population growth,

[21]Thomas Robert Malthus, *An Essay on the Principle of Population,* ed. Philip Appleman (New York: W. W. Norton & Company, 1976).

[22]*Economic Report of the President February 1990,* 329.

the birth control pill, is virtually useless to a noneducated population. To put it alchemically, no birth control method is even close to being an R-I-T, since none is user-transparent.

As examined in Chapter 4, the nations of the Third World are falling off the economic edge. They do not have the infrastructure necessary to use most of our technological resources; since they have very little of value to trade for what they need, few in our society are working on technological innovations that could be used with their limited resources. Our best and brightest Alchemists are busy developing better automobiles and high-definition television sets. The Third World nations, assuming they wanted and could afford these items, lack even the basic infrastructure—roads and electrical power—to use them.

These nations do have an abundance of certain basic raw materials that we once thought they would use to pay for the development of their infrastructure, but the value of these raw materials fell nearly 75 percent during just the first half of the last decade. And the future looks even worse. Owing to recent technological breakthroughs in alchemic processes for using and converting physical resources, the developed nations are entering a period in which they may not need just less raw materials from the Third World; rather, they may not need any at all. As discussed in Chapter 2, the actual demand for many raw materials is falling as fast or even faster than their price.

Ironically, the only hope for the Third World is far more of exactly what caused their current predicament: technology. In order to utilize almost any of our technological resources, they need to have an entire technological infrastructure—or develop new innovative products that are not dependent on such an infrastructure. For example, they need an entire transportation network to move their people and materials, or else need to develop vehicles that are not dependent on smooth roads. They need to have a network to distribute electrical power throughout their countries, or else develop new ways to efficiently produce electrical power wherever it is needed. And they need to be able to irrigate their farm produce and protect their crops from pests, or else develop crops that don't need much water and are immune to pests.

Fortunately, the major technological breakthroughs now in our laboratories hold great promise for the Third World. Recent breakthroughs in superconductivity may lead to magnetic levitation vehicles that ride above the ground, powered by super-efficient batteries and electric motors. Potential developments in cold fusion could lead to the ability to generate power everywhere from almost anything, even sea water. And already available genetically engineered plants require far less water and no pesticides because they are immune to pests. Moreover, we are no longer asking our scientists if these things are possible; we are asking them *when* we can have them.

Unfortunately, these breakthroughs may not come soon enough for the Third World; when they do come, they may not be applicable to the needs of less-developed countries. This is especially true now that the Third World no longer has the raw materials to pay for the development of the R-I-Ts they are able to use (a genetic laboratory today would find it much more profitable to develop a crop immune to pests in Montana rather than one immune to pests in Mozambique). What the world needs today is a technological version of the Peace Corps, where our best scientists volunteer to work entirely on developing R-I-Ts specifically applicable to the Third World.

> You gotta have a dream,
> if you don't have a dream,
> then how you gonna have your dream come true?[23]

In the alchemic world, where we have the power to create unlimited wealth, what we can accomplish is limited only by our dreams. In fact, it was the American dream itself, more than anything else, that made us the richest and most powerful nation on earth. We have the ability today to control our destiny; the question facing us now is, what will we do with this power?

In 1982, the United States embarked upon what has already become the longest peacetime economic expansion in history. More significantly, when we examine the underlying cause of this unprecedented expansion—that is, the implementation of technological advances—we can see that the United States, and the entire Western World, is entering a multidecade period of economic expansion of unfathomable proportions.

[23]Richard Rodgers and Oscar Hammerstein, "Happy Talk," *South Pacific*, 1958.

As for those who are being left behind, we have the ability to bring them into our alchemic world so that they, too, can share in the prosperity. Not only is it morally and ethically right that we should do this, but it is also in our economic best interests. Indeed, when we accomplish this noble objective, we may well become known not only as the richest and most powerful nation on earth but as, to paraphrase the words of our president, the kindest and gentlest as well.

The situation for the world's less developed nations is not as auspicious. But some of the most significant technological advances in the history of humankind—cold fusion, superconductivity, genetic engineering—may be just over the horizon. We can therefore hope that these imminent developments will allow the rest of the world to share in the wealth of the alchemic age.

As we enter the last decade of the twentieth century, more than just our promising economic future is in sight. We have finally reached the age that every would-be Alchemist has dreamed of from the beginning of time: the age when one person's gain is not another person's loss, when what we should do because it is morally right is exactly what we must do to increase our individual and societal wealth, when the only limit to what we can accomplish is what we can dream of accomplishing—the Age of Alchemy.

ACKNOWLEDGMENTS

THE ACKNOWLEDGMENTS for a theory that has taken 15 years to develop begin with members of my family.

First is my father, who left me in body in 1979, but who has never left my side in spirit. Next, but equally important, is my mother, whose optimistic Dr. Pangloss view of life led to the faith that there could be an alchemic economic theory. And last, but most important, there is my brother, Lee, who not only worked tirelessly on the manuscript, but who has also been my best friend, my college roommate, and almost everything else since we both graduated from Lehigh University together in 1974.

Then there are my teachers, whose dreams and aspirations achieve immortality through the students they touch. To them, I can only say that my lifelong goal is to inspire some of my students as so many of these teachers have inspired me. And my business partners—Jeff Juster, Steve Jarchow, and especially Alan May—have also taught me valuable lessons and have selflessly allowed me to shine because of their achievements. They have taught me the most important lesson of all—trust in one's fellow man.

Next is my first researcher, Brandon Williams, whose intellectual genius and spiritual purity proved invaluable in discovering the historical relationship between technology and economic progress. And I owe a great deal to my former editor at Simon & Schuster, Allan Mayer, and his assistant, Renee Vogel, who helped me get the theory on paper and finish the original proposal. Allan and Renee began working with me as professional colleagues but finished as true friends.

And throughout this process, as well as every other book I have or probably ever will write, has been my literary agent, Jan Miller, still known as "the dreammaker" to the many authors on whom she was the first one to take a chance.

Every project has its darkest hour from which the finished product usually emerges much stronger. The darkest hour for this project occurred in November 1989. Looking back, it is now clear what was missing—a chapter by chapter application of the theory to the most important issues of our lives. One very special individual, Jim Wade at Crown Publishers (who ultimately was to become my editor and the project's midwife), believed enough in the promise of an alchemic economic theory to bring it to fruition. To him, I will always be eternally grateful for his early faith in our project and in awe of his knowledge of so many facets of our lives.

It was also during this darkest hour that my friend Tony Meyer told me I should meet a potential researcher, a young woman who spoke Russian and was studying for her Ph.D. in economics. In A.D. 645 one of the early alchemists wrote that the alchemic secret of creating great wealth could not be obtained "by means of any knowledge unless it be through affection and gentle humility, a perfect and true love."[1] This woman, whose rare combination of humility with beauty and intelligence, brought to the project, and to my life, the true love that was needed for its completion.

To Donna Lynn Casey, to whom this book is dedicated, I can only say that I truly feel my inadequacies as a writer when I try to put on paper how much I love and respect you.

[1] Lee Stavenhagen, ed. and trans., *A Testament of Alchemy* (Hanover: The University Press of New England, 1974), 11.

SELECTED BIBLIOGRAPHY

Blaug, Mark. *Great Economists Before Keynes*. Cambridge: Cambridge University Press, 1986.

———. *Great Economists Since Keynes*. Cambridge: Cambridge University Press, 1985.

Bloom, Allan. *The Closing of the American Mind*. New York: Simon & Schuster, 1987.

Boorstin, Daniel J. *The Discoverers—A History of Man's Search to Know His World and Himself*. New York: Vintage Books, 1983.

Club of Rome. *The Limits to Growth*. New York: Universe Books, 1972.

Cohen, Rev. Dr. A. *The Soncino Chumash—The Five Books of Moses With Haphtaroth*. London: The Soncino Press, 1983.

Creveld, Martin Van. *Technology and War*. New York: The Free Press, 1989.

Dertouzos, Michael L., Richard K. Lester, and Robert M. Solow. *Made in America—Regaining the Productive Edge*. Cambridge, Mass.: MIT Press, 1989.

Dinnerstein, Leonard, and David Reimers. *Ethnic Americans: A History of Immigration and Assimilation*. New York: New York University Press, 1977.

Elegant, Robert. *Pacific Destiny: Inside Asia Today.* New York: Crown Publishers, 1990.

Erickson, Charlotte. *American Industry and the European Immigrant: 1860–1885.* Cambridge, Mass.: Harvard University Press, 1957.

Executive Office of the President. *Economic Report of the President— Transmitted to the Congress February 1990.* Washington: Government Printing Office, 1990.

————. Office of Management and Budget. *Historical Tables—Budget of the United States Government.* Washington: Government Printing Office, 1989.

————. Office of National Drug Control Policy. *National Drug Control Strategy.* Washington: Government Printing Office, 1990.

Fallows, James. *More Like Us.* Boston: Houghton Mifflin Co., 1989.

Frame, Donald M., trans. *Voltaire: Candide, Zadig and Selected Stories.* New York: New American Library, 1961.

Fulghum, Robert. *All I Really Need To Know I Learned In Kindergarten—Uncommon Thoughts On Common Things.* New York: Villard Books, 1988.

Galbraith, John Kenneth. *The Affluent Society.* 4th ed. New York: New American Library, 1958.

Gilder, George. *Microcosm: The Quantum Revolution in Economics and Technology.* New York: Simon and Schuster, 1989.

Glazer, Nathan. *The New Immigration: A Challenge to American Society.* San Diego: San Diego State University Press, 1988.

Gooch, James, Michael George, and Douglas Montgomery. *America Can Compete.* Dallas: The Institute of Business Technology, 1987.

Hawking, Stephen W. *A Brief History of Time.* New York: Bantam Books, 1988.

Hirsch, E. D., Jr. *Cultural Literacy—What Every American Needs To Know.* Boston: Houghton Mifflin Company, 1987.

Hughes, Thomas P. *American Genesis—A Century of Invention and Technological Enthusiasm.* New York: Viking Penguin, 1989.

Jowett, M. A., trans. *Plato's Republic.* New York: Modern Library, 1982.

Keynes, John Maynard. *The General Theory of Employment, Interest, and Money.* San Diego: Harcourt Brace Jovanovich Publishers, 1964.

Lemay, Michael C. *The Gatekeepers—Comparative Immigration Policy.* New York: Praeger Publishers, 1989.

Malthus, Thomas Robert. *An Essay on the Principle of Population.* Edited by Philip Appleman. New York: W.W. Norton & Company, 1976.

Pilzer, Paul Zane. "The Real Estate Business and Technological Obsolescence." *Real Estate Review* (Fall 1989): 30–33.

Pilzer, Paul Zane, with Robert Deitz. *Other People's Money.* New York: Simon & Schuster, 1989.

Redgrove, H. Stanley. *Alchemy: Ancient and Modern.* New Hyde Park, N.Y.: University Books, 1969.

Samuelson, Paul A., and William D. Nordhaus. *Economics,* 12th ed. New York: McGraw-Hill Book Company, 1985.

Schumpeter, Joseph A. *Capitalism, Socialism, and Democracy.* New York: Harper & Brothers Publishers, 1950.

Stavenhagen, Lee, ed. and trans. *A Testament of Alchemy.* Hanover, N.H.: University Press of New England, 1974.

U.S. Congress. Office of Technology Assessment (OTA). *Technology and the American Economic Transition: Choices for the Future.* Washington: Government Printing Office, 1988.

U.S. Department of Commerce. Bureau of the Census. *Statistical Abstract of the United States 1989.* 109th ed. Washington: Government Printing Office, 1989.

U.S. Department of Labor. Bureau of Labor Statistics. *Projections 2000*. Washington: Government Printing Office, 1988.

————. Employment Standards and Administration. *Opportunity 2000—Creative Affirmative Action Strategies for a Changing Workforce*. Washington: Government Printing Office, 1988.

Workforce 2000—Work and Workers for the Twenty-First Century. Indianapolis: Hudson Institute, 1987.

INDEX